THE GLORY OF EGYPT

I HATE ANTHONY PARKERS.

GRANDE PYRAMIDE DE KHÉOPS
THE GREAT PYRAMID OF CHEOPS

THE GLORY OF EGYPT

115 Photographs by
MICHEL AUDRAIN
Text and Notes by
SAMIVEL

With
ten Translations of original
Egyptian Texts

A Thames and Hudson Book
THE VANGUARD PRESS
NEW YORK

Translated by

J. E. MANCHIP WHITE

Monochrome plates printed in France by Ets Braun et Cie Mulhouse
Colour plates printed in France by l'Imprimerie Générale Grenoble
Text printed in Great Britain by Jarrold and Sons Ltd Norwich

CONTENTS

FOREWORD

THIS BOOK IS THE OUTCOME of a visit to Egypt in 1954 by a team of French documentary-film makers, under the leadership of M. Samivel.

"Samivel"—who has paid England the compliment of taking his pseudonym from *The Pickwick Papers*—is well known in France as artist, author and film-producer. He has made a name for himself as a traveller, and his voyages have taken him to places as far afield as Greenland and the Sahara. Mountains in particular have always held a fascination for him, and in 1952 a colour-film called *Mountains and Marvels* which he shot on one of his expeditions was awarded first prize at an international film festival. In addition, he has written and illustrated a number of books of his own.

During this last expedition to Egypt, M. Samivel and his associates journeyed along the whole course of the Nile from the lush Mediterranean Delta in the north to the rocky uplands of the Sudan in the south. While M. Samivel himself was primarily engaged with the colour-camera, M. Michel Audrain, his associate, compiled the greater part of the series of photographs that follow. They remain faithful to the spirit of Robert Flaherty that informs M. Samivel's work in the field of the cinema, and constitute a remarkable by-product of a remarkable undertaking.

To the magnificent pictorial record compiled by M. Audrain, M. Samivel has contributed an introductory essay and a series of notes on the individual plates. As one might expect, the essay is stimulating, and demonstrates clearly the author's preoccupation with the mystery of mountains. It also displays his marked practical bent, and shows the eager, questing quality of mind that has sent him voyaging to all quarters of the globe.

In his provocative essay on the significance of the pyramids, the achievements of Egyptian art and the inner meaning of the ancient civilization of the Nile Valley, M. Samivel is everywhere at pains to emphasize that he is not a professional Egyptologist. It is not his intention to try to make a profound contribution to academic Egyptology. No, he is by training an artist, a master of modern visual techniques, and his aim is to convey to his reader, with all due modesty and diffidence, a tithe of the sense of wonder and admiration that his visit to Egypt aroused in him. And strikingly well, in the opinion of the translator, he manages to convey it. Without pedantry, he brings to the study of Ancient Egypt a fresh and practised eye, a first-hand knowledge of artistic procedures, and a keen comparative experience of the ways-of-life of a dozen different peoples.

The form of his essay will perhaps be more familiar to French than to English readers. It belongs to that category of widely-ranging discourses on art and human existence which are a feature of French literature, and of which the outstanding modern example is Malraux's *Voix du Silence*. It is not confined to the strict and rather staid conventions which are ordinarily imposed on English writers when they employ this particular *genre*. M. Samivel feels himself free, partly because of accepted French literary custom and partly because he is a self-confessed amateur in the sphere of Egyptian archaeology, to comment generally on the art, architecture and religious preoccupations of the Ancient Egyptians. None the less, the translator would like to point out that M. Samivel's knowledge of Egypt is by no means as superficial as he would lead us to suppose. His essay, despite its numerous delightful and provocative digressions, presents a neat outline account of the rise and fall of the once mighty Two Lands of the Nile Valley. His commentary on the plates mingles historical fact with artistic perception in the same admirable fashion.

Between the essay and the commentary, M. Samivel has inserted a number of pieces of Ancient Egyptian prose and verse, which serve as a graceful interlude between the two more serious sections of the book. The translator has attempted to render these specimens of ancient literature, which do not in the present instance call for textbook treatment, into good modern English, instead of into the stiff Biblical English which is so often employed. It is surely doing Ancient Egyptian literature no service to make it appear more rigid and fossilized than is necessary. There are indications that in many of their literary modes the Ancient Egyptians were in the habit of using all manner of colloquialisms and racy idioms. It is possible to retain the dignity of the original passages without making them virtually unreadable.

In conclusion, it seems fair to say that M. Samivel would not mind if we were to draw special attention to the superb photographs that form the backbone of the book. They are in a sense its chief *raison d'être*, and they offer us a faithful and moving account of the visible remains, both humble and heroic in scale, of what is perhaps the greatest and most enigmatic civilization that has so far contributed to the tale of mankind.

J. E. MANCHIP WHITE

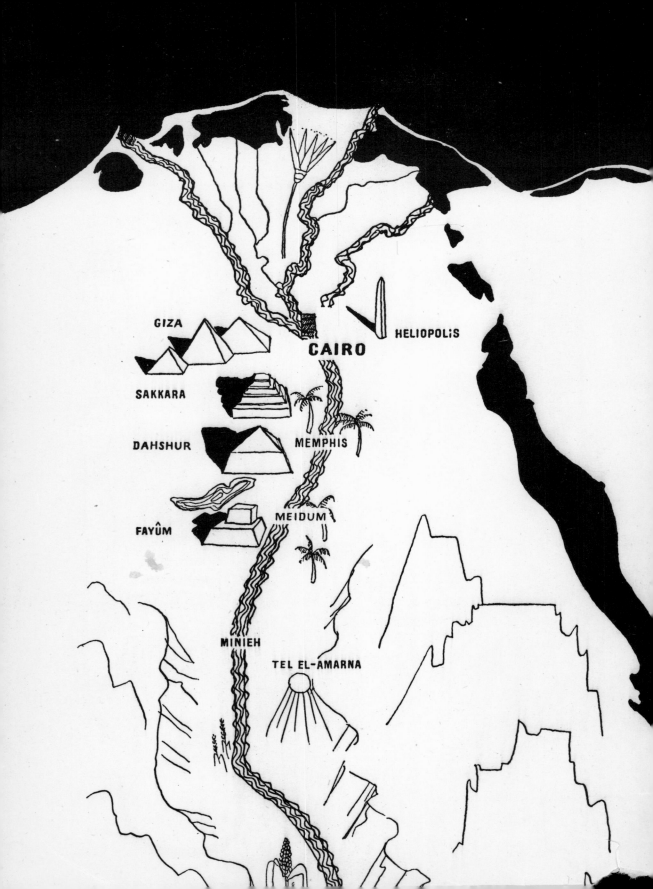

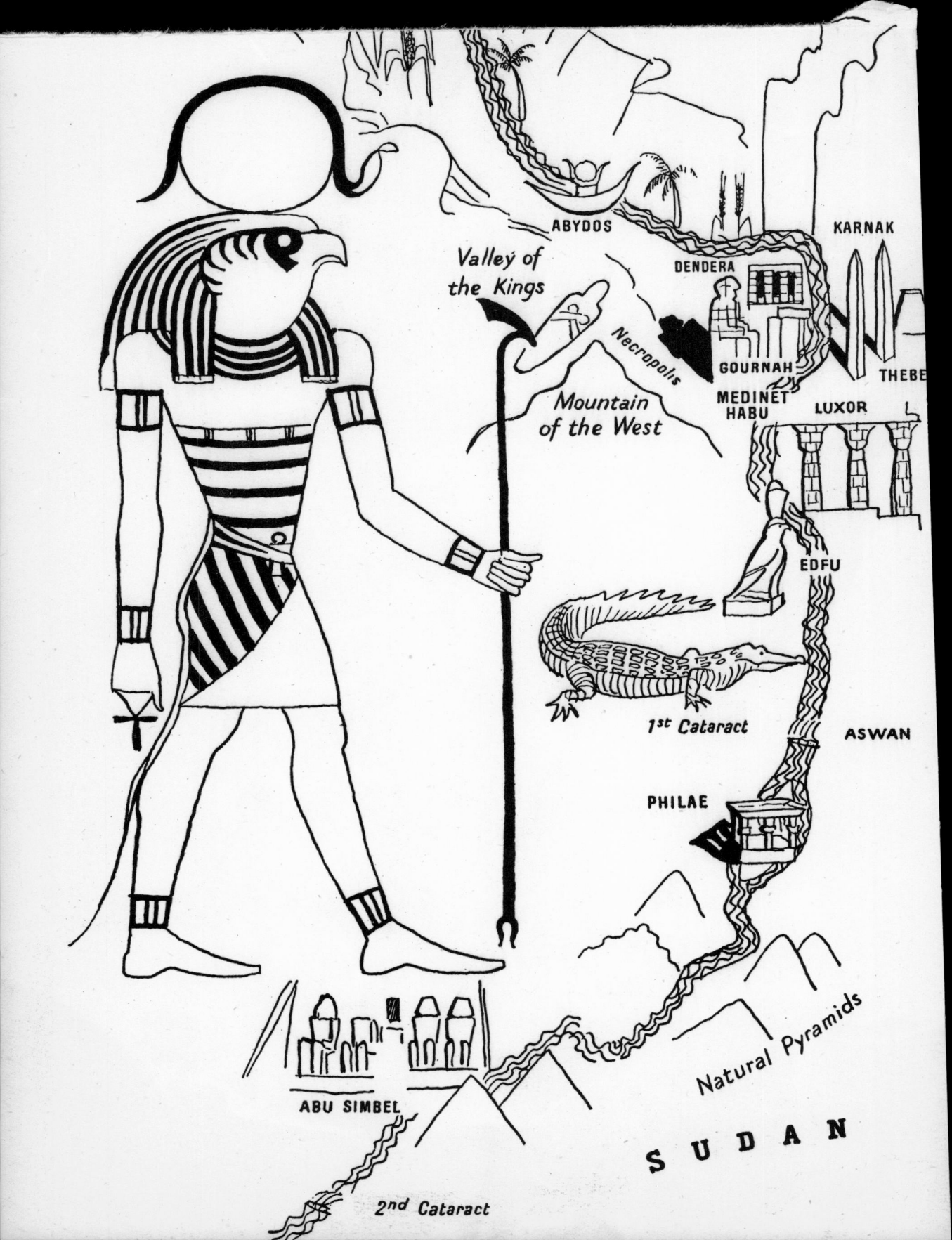

THE GLORY OF EGYPT

THERE CAME AN EPOCH when Christianity—possibly wearying of metaphysical exploration—looked around and took note of the existence of the great world, and thereupon discovered new reasons for living. It was then that thousands of adventurers, devoured by a gargantuan thirst for knowledge, hurled themselves like shock-troops upon the citadel of brute matter. In this period, which we call the Renaissance, the study of classical antiquity once again became the fashion. As a result of a revolution in Western society and in Western philosophy, the exploration of heavenly and terrestrial space was intensified, in laboratories and observatories. At the same time, other men were travelling in all directions to explore the seas, the barbaric shadows of the jungle, the distant mountain tops. The study of the physical world reached such a pitch of intensity that a few despondent spirits went so far as to state that the taking of the Grand Inventory was practically finished.

Fortunately, this was not so. The knowledge of the universe is an ideal to pursue, rather than a reality to be attained. Every age and every individual observer seizes upon a different facet of Truth, which always remains ultimately out of range. Only great temerity, or the current passion for intellectual comfort, can derive any satisfaction from the notion of a slow accumulation of expertly-quarried and beautifully-squared stones from which will rise, on the distant morrow, the Temple of Science and Virtue. This view does not take into account the fact that there is a Dimension of which twentieth-century man has lost nearly all knowledge. He is as ignorant of this Dimension as his Stone Age ancestor would have been if he had been confronted by the Yellow River, Cape Horn, Easter Island,

Ruwenzori or the Aleutians. This Dimension, whose perspectives fade away into the immeasurable distance, is the Dimension of Time. It is encircled by the two symmetrical oceans of the Past and the Future, which swirl ceaselessly around the flimsy raft upon which mankind floats aimlessly along.

Like the immensity of Space, the immensity of Time brings with it a sensation of anguish. It is against this unbearable feeling of anguish that our conservative instincts urge us to erect breastworks. Where the Future is concerned, for the sake of our peace of mind we have elaborated the myth of Progress. The myth is a good working hypothesis, and it appears to produce universal satisfaction. As for the Past, ordinary people prefer to ignore it altogether; but those of a livelier mentality have invented the idea of History, which is an effort on the part of mankind to make a raid into the domain of the Third Dimension. The old phrase "Unexplored" is often found covering large white expanses on early maps; but these twin oceans of Time are surely infinitely more mysterious than the geographical blanks on ancient charts. In these oceans lie concealed such fundamental discoveries as the first lesson in navigation and the first control of fire.

According to recent estimates, it may be as much as a million years since man was born and since he began to think. The investigations of archaeologists can carry us back, with a fair degree of accuracy, for some thirty thousand years. Beyond this point there is little more than silence and shadow. We therefore have an imperfect knowledge of about three per cent of the actual history of our species. What happened during the great lost aeons? What adventures, what wanderings, what dramas, what sufferings, what exaltations? What civilizations came successively into being in different parts of the world, then were snuffed out and superseded by others, and by still others again? Of these matters we are almost entirely ignorant. Millions, milliards of human beings like ourselves have lived, worked, fought, taken their pleasure in the course of hundreds of centuries. And we know little or nothing about them. Is it possible that one day we shall learn something more substantial about their mode of life? If the atom bomb leaves modern students enough time to explore the bottom of the ocean and the depths of the glacial ice, where the answers to their questions may lie concealed, will we discover a fraction more about our earliest ancestors? Or will we learn nothing of any value? In any case, the sweet and simple hypothesis held by the happy inhabitants of the nineteenth century, according to which humanity marches ever onwards towards the Promised Land, has now been relegated to the scrap-heap. The theory of Evolution is not held as tenaciously as once it was; but it may be that, although human society undergoes successive periods of progression and regression, and is subject to innumerable oscillations, the tide of each new civilization mounts a little higher than the preceding one. That is as far as one can go without confusing myth with sober fact.

When we turn our attention towards the yawning horizons of the Past, we are like travellers who arrive on the shore of an unknown ocean. In the far distance, a few small islands can be descried on the surface of the water. The islands include the Isle of the Incas, the Isle of the Sumerians, and the Isle of the Egyptians. But between them and us lie vast reefs of pre-history. And there is nothing beyond the islands but the empty sweep of the horizon. In all directions, wherever one looks, the landscape is covered by the mists of oblivion.

We have spoken of the Isle of Egypt. If we substitute the desert for the sea, Egypt is nothing less than an island. And what a strange island it is! It is five hundred miles long and only twelve miles wide, and its shape is determined by the course of the great river which created it—by means of silt washed down in the course of many millennia. In the south, the waters of the river surge mysteriously out of the arid depths of the African continent; in the north, it spreads across the Delta like the giant flower of one of the clumps of papyrus upon its banks. To east and west there is nothing: nothing, that is, of any use to man. There is nothing to east or west but the burning monotony of an ancient, terrible geological struggle which bent

13

and warped the primary rocks. And away to infinity stretch the twin empires of silence and barrenness.

The only visitor to these desolate confines is the sun. Every morning, huge and smoking, it bounds into view between the peaks of the mountains. Then, after its long journey across the waters of the heavenly Nile, it sinks slowly into the Libyan steppes, into the subterranean dwellings of death and night.

It was in this extraordinary locality, as shut-in as a coffin, that man first found his settled home. Man and the gods settled down on this long straight strip of fertile soil, which apparently contained the whole of the physical world. Through it ran not only the mighty river, but Time itself.

This first settlement took place in the fabulous, confused times between the Old and New Stone Ages. Very little is known about the original races that came together in the narrow valley. It seems likely that during this long stretch of time the representatives of some Mediterranean civilization took root in the Delta. From the Delta, they groped their way slowly upstream, and there came into contact with other and more primitive tribes of an indigenous origin. After many vicissitudes and ups-and-downs that the sands have obliterated, slowly there came into existence two distinct kingdoms of Upper and Lower Egypt. This dualism was created by the form of the country itself. There was a tendency towards homogeneity imposed by the unity of the great river, and an opposing tendency, because of the contrast between Upper Egypt and the Delta, that was hostile to unification. At one and the same time the Nile was the cause of the unity and disunity of Ancient Egypt, whose political history is symbolized by the Double Crown its princes were later to wear.

History furnishes few examples of geographical determinism as striking as Egypt. The direct and preponderating influence of their natural surroundings affected the Ancient Egyptians in many different ways. This country of theirs, strictly delimited by the surrounding desert, was characterized by a small number of cosmic presences that always remained the same. These were the river, the verdure, the nourishing silt, the characteristic fauna. There was also the great fiery orb that traversed the

14

entire span of the visible world, the immobile deserts of silence, and the red sand.

The river not only nourished the bodies of the people who were to dwell along its banks for two hundred generations, it also conditioned their ways of thought, their conception of life and the universe. Egyptian mythology, like Egyptian hieroglyphs and Egyptian architecture, bears the distinctive marks of its locale. And it is precisely in the degree to which the members of this great nation knew how to express themselves according to the strict conditions laid down by Nature itself, that their works attained the peak of art. The genius of Egypt was never subordinated to a fatal facility or to any dispersion of its powers: it was always itself. This is surely a lesson for us today, when taste has become so hopelessly eclectic. The genius of Egypt is like the mighty Nile, canalized between its two eternal rocky walls. Locked within this narrow, immovable bed, it pours out its force with a power that, at a distance of dozens of centuries, in the era of armoured-cars and mechanical robots, still astounds us with the sight of the great blocks of stone it has thrown upwards towards the sky.

This land is a land of paradox and brutal contrast. The fields of har- vested corn merge into burning wastes. The furnace of the sun is reflected in the mild waters of the river, whose inexhaustible waters gush out daily upon soil which for countless centuries has not known a single drop of dew. Above the thin green plain of the valley looms the gigantic bulk of solemn buildings, the bulk of dumb cliffs which nothing has changed from the beginning of the world. The landscape of Egypt is an incorruptible vista of rocks, stamped out by the punch of the Almighty on the blinding blue enamel of the sky. The landscape is beyond pity. It is a landscape of alti- tude, of metaphysical void. The enormous Nothingness which surrounds every quarter of the Egyptian landscape, the implacable confrontation of the fluent forms of life with the harsh immortality of the rocks, brings to mind with dramatic intensity the eternal problem of life and death, of the transitory and the absolute. It was to this country that man, fragile and menaced by many dangers, clung as his chosen land. It seemed to him the fruit of a double and constant miracle, the miracle of the Sun and the

River, both surging inexplicably out of primordial solitude, renewing themselves for the sole benefit of the blessed Valley and the frail creatures who lived there.

The Ancient Egyptian was the most religious of all men. His heart was swollen simultaneously by pride and fear. Was he not the focal-point of so much mysterious solicitude on the part of a transcendant Finalism? Was he not surrounded fraternally by many other living species, species whom he believed were also the sign and manifestation of a superhuman Energy? He drank deep of the passion for eternity, a passion as melancholy as it was inexhaustible. For generation after generation, he skirted the ageless, fathomless gulfs of the endless deserts. He was squeezed as though in a vice between the brooding silences of east and west.

Other civilizations were polarized around different ideas. The Assyrians gave themselves up to the cult of war-like expansion, the Incas to social organization, the Romans to political unification, the Christians to religious proselytism. No doubt the ideal of the Ancient Egyptians underwent many changes, for its apparent immobility is deceptive; but it appears to have been marked throughout its history by a stubborn, heroic battle against the transitory Present, against death, ultimately against the very appearance of things. For countless centuries, the members of a single nation sought to come close to the immortal gods, to identify themselves with them, to traverse the river of destruction and the night of death. And it was by means of the incredible pertinacity with which they pursued this crystalline, incorruptible dream, which is the dream of Mankind itself, that they achieved grandeur—and not only grandeur, but wisdom.

The sands have yielded a confused mass of relics that date from this early period. There are flint implements, palettes covered with mysterious messages, vases cut from solid stone. All are equally admirable in design and technical execution. Then, on the strong tide of the Nile, the historical dynasties are borne down to us. And at that point, it seems to our astounded gaze that the art of Ancient Egypt bounds, completely formed, on to the historical stage, fifty-two centuries before our era. The impeccable rendering of the falcon on the palette of Narmer [Plate 11] could only be the finished product of a tradition which had already outgrown its period of tentative groping. There is nothing that could be added or subtracted from the line and volume of the falcon of Narmer. It resembles, indeed, the great falcon of Edfu; and this shows that the same plastic ideal was capable of inspiring two artists situated at opposite ends of the historical scroll of Ancient Egypt. This fact is in itself indicative of the vitality of Egyptian thought.

This fundamental identity of style is an artistic manifestation brought about by some unknown agency. Each inflection of line, each rendering of volume, each touch of colour is a Sign. It is the direct outcome of a metaphysical reality emerging in the world of artistic form. It shows that the thought which lies behind it had already been defined in essential outline during and before the onset of the first recorded dynasties. All the same, we must repeat that this should not be taken as evidence that the Ancient Egyptians were the victims of a sort of mental paralysis. This is a hasty judgment, to which many persons who study this fascinating civilization are prone. Just as the grain of a certain plant differs in structure from another grain, and develops in a definite direction towards its own biological fulfilment, so the so-called "archaising" proclivities of the Ancient Egyptians fulfil themselves with the same fertile dynamism, which from the beginning of their civilization was confined to the strict pattern of a particular representation of the universe.

And this dimension of Time, of which we have been speaking, has it anything to do with us? How can we judge? These immense vistas of time, this span of epochs, still have the power to frighten us. We have become the victims of our own terrified vision of things, which causes many people to flee in panic from the idea of the Present. This flight is the peculiar vice of a century which is devoured by the leprosy of speed. In the way that there is an individual difference in the pattern of growth of individuals, may there also be a different individual pattern discernible in the evolution of human roots?

Already in the pre-Thinite period, and even in the proto- and pre-historic periods that preceded it, tombs whose complicated structure demonstrate a definite notion of the cosmos and of destiny have been found. These early tombs and sanctuaries do not appear to have been modified in any essential way during the course of the three thousand five hundred years that followed. The whole arrangement of the funerary cult, of which we shall be speaking a little later on, can be discerned from a study of these primitive graves or *mastabas*, already surmounted by the rectangular tumulus from which springs the whole idea of the artificial mountain. The first important tomb of this character which has so far been discovered is that of Nebekta, of the First "Thinite" Dynasty, who lived about 3200 B.C. It seems to have possessed a stepped superstructure. Here, in miniature, can already be detected the formidable pile of Sakkara.

The Pyramid of Sakkara is the first known pyramid. It dates from the reign of the Pharaoh Zoser, of the Third Dynasty, and is the work of Imhotep, the first architect whose name is known to history. It represents the final outcome of a number of increases in height erected upon the ground-plan of a mastaba. It originally consisted of six steps or terraces, culminating in a platform on the summit that formed the seventh step.

The Pharaoh Snofru, of the Fourth Dynasty, was also a remarkable builder. He seems to have built two, perhaps three, pyramids, each in a different architectural style. The Pyramid of Meidum was a step pyramid like Zoser's, probably with seven steps, and as at Sakkara the steps were separated by solid walls. Thus the monument did not offer any way of access to its summit, unlike those other artificial mountains, the Sumerian ziggurats. Snofru's pyramid, moreover, is a work that is perfectly balanced in its proportions, and the hypothesis that it was merely designed to be the kernel of a "regular" pyramid which was never finished is almost certainly unsound. One can also say the same of this monarch's second pyramid, the so-called Bent Pyramid of Dahshur. This pyramid possesses four smooth

18

faces which show a sudden change of angle two-thirds of the way up. This strange appearance might very well suggest that the original plan on which it was built had to be changed because of an error of calculation during the course of its erection. However that may be, the great innovation which is shown by the Bent Pyramid resides in two factors: firstly, there is a total suppression of the technique of building by steps; secondly, it adopts the form of the pyramid proper, that is to say, it has four right-angled faces of smooth masonry converging into a point or pyramidion. The first pyramid proper is actually Snofru's third pyramid, the so-called Great Pyramid of Dahshur, which henceforward was to serve as the pattern for the pyramids which followed it.

North of the plateau of Dahshur, the isolated peak of the Step Pyramid at Sakkara can be seen rising from the desert. Then, far away on the horizon, can be viewed the great range formed by three peaks of world-wide fame, the Alps of Giza. These are the pyramids of the Pharaohs Cheops, Chephren, and Mycerinus, together with several other pyramids of smaller dimensions. They are the work of the Pharaohs of the Fourth Dynasty. In volume, the dimensions of two of them are the largest of any buildings that have ever been built. The Great Pyramid of Cheops was known to the ancients as "the Shining One". It was originally nearly five hundred feet high, although the later destruction of the monuments of Ancient Egypt by the Arabs, who used them as a source of stone for their own buildings, makes it almost impossible to give accurate measurements in these matters. The Pyramid of Chephren was slightly smaller, but the angles of its faces were steeper, and in some ways it has a more dynamic appearance than the Great Pyramid. From the point of view of absolute altitude, it is actually higher than that of Cheops, and it was the Pyramid of Chephren and not the Pyramid of Cheops which was known as the Great Pyramid in ancient times. The third pyramid, the Pyramid of Mycerinus, is consider-ably smaller than the other two, being originally only two hundred and eighteen feet high. Its Egyptian name was "the Heavenly One". In their pristine state, the three pyramids were covered with a smooth dressing of limestone blocks, which covered the whole surface of the four faces and made the building completely inaccessible. In the humble opinion of the writer, this fact is important for the true understanding of buildings of this type.

There are other pyramids or groups of pyramids of less distinction on the soil of Egypt. They include the Pyramids of Abu Roash, Abusir, North and South Sakkara, and Lisht. They are all situated on the west bank of the river, and thus form a sort of artificial prolongation of the mountains of the Libyan chain. These extraordinary buildings have always gripped the imagination of visitors. They have provoked mountains of books and theories, either reasonable or fantastic, or else downright comic. The serious excavation which has now been carried on for more than a century has proved in every case that pyramids always contain the mummies and coffins of royal persons. Such relics have sometimes been found, although the royal resting-places were usually violated long before the onset of the Christian era. In view of the results of these excavations, it has usually been taken for granted that the pyramids were wholly and exclusively giant mausoleums, the product of imaginations devoured with inordinate pride. In addition to the classical theories, there has always been a spate of books given up to speculations of the most diverse nature. Some of them are Biblical, others occult, others prophetic. The prophetic theories are generally based on the internal or external measurements of pyramids, matters which, as we indicated above, are bound to be speculative. Most theories of this sort are founded almost entirely on measurements of the Great Pyramid, a fact which serves to indicate their essentially unreal nature: as we have just seen, it was not the Pyramid of Cheops but the Pyramid of Chephren which was regarded as the Great Pyramid by the Egyptians themselves. The many other pyramids in Egypt are never considered, although any hypothesis on the nature of these prodigious monuments must clearly take all the available facts into account.

It may perhaps seem extremely presumptuous on the part of the writer, who is in no way a professional Egyptologist, to dare to formulate his own theory on a subject which has been hotly debated by men of great learning and intelligence. But it has always been the privilege of even the humblest among us to submit their ideas modestly to the attention of the specialist, and to plead the legitimate benefit of historical doubt. The writer, therefore, begs leave to bring forward some speculations of his own on the precise function of pyramids, on the origin of their architectural style, and on the technique of construction utilized by their builders. He has attempted to approach these thorny problems from a somewhat different angle than his many worthy predecessors. He considers that the key to this problem resides in the symbolism of altitude, which has interested him for many years. This symbolism has appealed to many men in many places at many times.

It seems reasonable to suppose that everyone would agree with this very simple definition: *Pyramids are artificial mountains.* Once this has been said, it would seem that one has said everything.

But to admit that pyramids are artificial mountains is to broach a problem of universal significance, a problem which may have more to do with psychology than with architecture and archaeology. In pursuit of what beliefs, what ideas about the world, did a particular human society apply its intellectual genius and physical powers to the erection of monuments which in shape and elevation resemble mountains? Why were the Sumerian ziggurats brought into existence, the high temples of the Incas, the tumuli of the Scandinavians, the cathedrals of the Christians? Why, in fact, are there pyramids in Egypt? May not the reply to such general questions contain the solution of a particular problem?

It will be necessary, from the outset, to make a brief incursion into the strange, dim universe of ancient cosmogony. It is only by taking account of the ideas which our ancient ancestors possessed about the world around them that we can attempt to come to some understanding of their works and the ends which they pursued. Long before the first great voyages of exploration, and the invention of those instruments which enabled the

21

theory or account of origins of universe

traveller to fix his precise position in any part of the world and pinpoint the location of the earth itself in relation to the universe—long before this, mankind possessed an instinctive horror of chaos. Men have always sought to give some semblance of order to the mysterious world by which they are surrounded. In consequence, they have invented a number of theories which are sometimes worked out with remarkable logic in spite of fundamentally illogical premises. No doubt these theories are almost anthropomorphic in tendency, but they enable mankind to escape from the terror of the Unknown. The architectural scheme by which the great globe itself was constructed is naturally one of mankind's principle sources of interest, and in the early world it gave rise to a whole throng of different cosmogonies. These ancient theories vary from one early civilization to the next, but they appear to possess certain elements in common. The first is that the world appears to consist in most cases of three superimposed levels: the terrestrial, the subterranean, the celestial. The first level is the domain of the living, the second of the dead, the third of transcendent superhuman personages—spirits, gods or demi-urges. Each of these cosmic layers was conceived, in its simplest form, as a flat plane.

This conception would have remained vague and aimless if it had not been supported by the invention of an axis, which served both as the central pivot of the entire system and as the material link between the three cosmic planes. The axis also served as the pillar of heaven, although there are other, more complex theories which assign this role to boundary-stones or columns situated at the four cardinal points of the compass.

We ought to attempt to define more precisely the nature of the central axis and the heavenly pillars. Sometimes the axis took the form of a huge "cosmic tree", with its roots plunged deep into the subterranean depths beneath, its upper branches brushing the empyrean. An example is the tree Yggdrasil, found in Germanic mythology. At other times, this triple role of axis, pillar, and link is assigned to a mountain, hill, or even simple mound.

We have thus summed up what might be described as the vertical aspect of primitive cosmogonies, in which the earth itself is regarded as a

22

flat plate existing on a horizontal plane. Thus, if there are mountains on the horizon, they are likely to be regarded as the columns of heaven and the boundary-stones of the habitable world. And beneath them lies the ocean of unformed chaos.

On this primary cosmogony a second system, of solar origin, is sometimes superimposed. The solar cosmogony is based on the visible arrangement and movement of the stars in general, and the sun in particular, during the course of the day. The mountains or the eastern horizon are regarded as the territory of the rising sun, while the mountains or western horizon are the domain of the setting sun. Therefore, by assimilation with the sun itself, and with its apparent death every evening, the west has become the abode of the dead.

In accordance with a universal human agreement, stemming from an early view of the nature of the Above and the Below, the celestial regions were given up to transcendent and, by extension, sacred beings. Deification was also bestowed on all material objects connected or in contact with the sky. This was particularly so in the case of mountains, which were considered to be either gods or the dwelling-places of gods. At length, mountains even became regarded as a link or ladder between the land of men and the heavenly habitation of the gods. And this point brings us back to the theory of the central axis.

The oldest dream of humanity, which has never been realized—despite the modern invention of aircraft—is the dream of being able to make one's way to the celestial regions, or at least to be able to approach them. Even in the twentieth century, it still persists in the form of ancient linguistic metaphors and images, and also in a sort of ascensional neo-mysticism. The most obvious example is the Christian Ascension, of which there are echoes in all religions. The notion can be found on a smaller scale, but in a form which is still materially effective, in the rites performed by witch-doctors or shamans in many parts of the world. As a rule, ascension to heaven is the prerogative of initiates and hierophants; but it is often believed that in some far-distant past it was possible for all men to ascend to or descend from heaven at will. Because of some primal fault, however, the

23

bridges were cut, and the celestial voyage was henceforward forbidden, except for a few privileged persons. Henceforward, men were condemned to cast envious glances at the skies, and only to go thither with great difficulty.

The powerful and universal attraction of the heavens has had incalculable consequences on the history of civilization; and it will continue to do so even in the coming epoch of interplanetary travel. It has directly affected the form of many of the palaces, temples, or monuments built by "primitive" societies. These buildings, in accordance with the theory of the central axis, were supposed to be able to lift men up, either literally or else by magical transference, to the centre of the universe. The centre of the universe was understood to mean the geographical point that presented the maximum of cosmic content, the point that pierced the three levels, serving as a means of intercommunication between them. This point would be vibrating with celestial energy, energy of a mingled spiritual and material nature. But the buildings were not only the means of lifting men up: they were also identified with this axis itself and also in many cases with the Primordial Cosmic Mountain. A large number were even considered to be artificial reproductions of the mythical Mountain of Creation, and their style of architecture conformed in many respects to this conception. The same idea is mirrored in the building of our own Christian cathedrals. In France, one finds it in the steeples of little village churches, and even in the Eiffel Tower itself, which may not altogether fancifully be considered the central axis of Paris, in opposition to the domes of Montmartre.

In civilizations, apparently less highly evolved than Ancient Egypt from the mystical viewpoint, such as the Assyrian, Babylonian, or Aztec, the temple-mountain sought to do no more than embody the primitive idea of a ladder reaching the celestial regions in the form of a gigantic stone stairway. The temple-mountain therefore consisted of a series of ramps or steps, and at the summit, the part of the monument closest to the sky, were performed the most important religious ceremonies and sacrifices. The idea of reaching heaven by means of an artificial mountain can be traced in the Bible, in the story of the Tower of Babel, which was none other than the

24

ziggurat of the city of Babylon. At a more advanced stage of religious awareness, the old formula of the step-ladder was realized in an architectural form that was no more than remotely suggestive of a staircase. And at a further stage still, the monument itself was merely regarded as an abstract spiritual symbol.

Once the ancients had hit upon the notion of the Central Cosmic Mountain, and had attributed this great primordial form by magical extension to all their monuments, it was only logical to choose so sacred a place for the bestowal of their dead. It was precisely in this sacred spot that the dead person, whether he had been deified or not, would find the most favourable conditions for reaching heaven, and for benefiting to the greatest possible extent from the flux of celestial and solar energy. It is not difficult to understand why so rare a privilege should have remained for many centuries the prerogative of royalty, or was preserved for a select handful of courtiers, priests, and noblemen. Here again we may detect this immemorial tradition in our own cathedrals and basilicas, where the remains of favoured persons are placed within the hallowed precincts, while the mass of ordinary beings, however devout, are deposited in the cemeteries which are clustered about the monument. In exactly the same way, the mastabas of the Early Empire are grouped around the focal-point provided by the royal pyramids.

In the light of what we have been saying, the problem of the pyramid assumes a different guise. We can already comprehend that the pyramid is not an isolated architectural phenomenon which bears no relation to other comparable architectural achievements. We can see that it is con-nected with a vast body of religious belief, in which it plays its own particular part. This leads us to further important considerations. In the first place, it appears likely that the artificial mountain-range of the pyramids, stretching from Lisht in the south to Abu Roash in the north, and begin-ning at the very point where the range of the real mountains of Libya begins to die away, suggests the idea that the pyramids were intended to be a sort of artificial prolongation of the natural mountain-barrier. This part-natural, part-artificial barrier constituted the frontier assigned by Egyptian mythology to the realm of the dead. Where Nature failed to provide a suitable mountain-barrier, the Egyptians thereupon provided one with their own hands. A singular fact reinforces this interpretation of the function of pyramids. When the religious centre of Egypt was transferred from the Delta to the city of Thebes, it was at the foot of the so-called Mountain of the West, which possessed the natural outline of a pyramid and was considered to be the abode of a powerful goddess, that the great funerary temples with their royal hypogeum and royal necropolis were built. Again, with the exception of the late and degenerate pyramids built by the negro kings of the Sudan at Napata and Meroë, all the pyramids of Egypt were constructed on the left or west bank of the river Nile: that is to say, on the bank where the sun appeared to set, and which was therefore considered to be the resting-place of the dead. The consistent choice of this locale could not have been due to chance: it is associated with mortuary-buildings in general, and coincides with the most reasonable interpretation of the purpose of the royal tombs. Since ancient cosmogonies usually considered the mountains of the west as the tomb of the sun, their identification with the tomb of human beings is not surprising. In any case, it is reinforced by the identification of the dead and resurrected Pharaoh with the sun itself.

The architecture of the pyramids furnishes a number of interesting clues about their function. To begin with, it is possible that not enough emphasis has been laid on the singular fact that the pyramids were *solid masses of stone*. The normal function of architecture is to enclose open spaces between a given number of walls. This is certainly not the case with the pyramids, or with the first mastabas of the Early Empire from which they were derived. The whole point of the pyramid was not to create hollow, enclosed spaces, but a solid volume of stone. The constructors of pyramids were trying to make a faithful copy of a natural form. They were trying to build an artificial mountain, with its own artificial corridors and caverns. It may be possible to deduce from these facts that, at some very remote epoch, the ancestors of the peoples who later came together in the Nile Valley inhabited a mountainous region, and were originally accustomed to placing their dead in natural caves in the mountains.

We must now make an observation whose significance will not escape the reader. It is this: There exist on the soil of Egypt a number of pyramids which were actually formed by Nature herself. The traveller who goes by boat to Upper Egypt, and sails from Aswan to Wadi Halfa in the Sudan, can see for himself that on both banks of the Nile there are dozens of natural pyramidal forms, emerging in a bizarre fashion from the sands of the desert. They are derived from rocky outcrops, the vestigial remains of geological strata planed down by the process of erosion. The likeness of these outcrops to the man-made pyramids of Lower Egypt is striking. They are roughly the same height, and the inclination of their faces is approximately the same angle. It may be noted that the angle of inclination of the faces of the architectural pyramid is not unlike the angle of a heap of boulders, the shape of which is determined by the weight of stone, a formation which helps to give it exceptional solidity. Another resemblance between the natural and artificial pyramid resides in its actual appearance as it stands silhouetted against the desert horizon. Again, because of the superimposition of geological strata of different degrees of density, certain of these natural pyramids consist of veritable steps, as at Sakkara, while others resemble in their outline the shape of the Bent Pyramid at Dahshur; and others have four plain faces and a quadrangular base, as at Giza. Any visitor to these lonely regions can verify these observations for himself.

It is not unnatural to suppose that the first designers of the pyramid were perfectly aware of this natural architecture of Upper Egypt, because of the expeditions which they themselves had made there, or even because their early ancestors had actually inhabited these inhospitable regions. From this supposition it is merely a step to propose that the sight of these natural mountains originally set in train the pyramidal idea. There are certainly less feasible explanations.

The first pyramid ever built, the Step Pyramid at Sakkara, was built, like the Pyramid at Meidum, in a series of stages. It reproduced the ancient theme of the heavenly ladder. Rituals based on this theme are still practised, as we have mentioned, by the shamans, sorcerers, and medicine-men of Central Asia, Australia, and elsewhere. The fact that it was physically impossible to climb the steps of these pyramids indicates that already, at this early date, the structure had no more than a purely symbolic value. Even this symbolic value of the ladder disappeared completely with the subsequent erection of pyramids with smooth faces. Henceforward only the spirit of faith was able to ascend these shining and inaccessible walls, to mount towards the nuptial point where the four faces of the building disappeared into the azure heavens. At this date the entire monument attained, by means of its geometrical discipline, a crystalline, superhuman purity. It became, in effect, a gigantic mound of rock-crystal, and it was even given an appearance of opacity by the dancing streams of sunlight reflected from its surface of smooth limestone. It is impossible to imagine a material form that could symbolize so effectively, and with such architectural simplicity, the ancient aspiration of mankind to reach a heavenly abode and to become identified with the sun.

The pure geometrical conception of the pyramid haunted the imagination of the Ancient Egyptians. During the centuries that followed its introduction, it reappeared in a number of different variants. These included the *benben*, the miniature pyramid that crowned the solar temples of Heliopolis, and the obelisk, which was nothing more than a pyramid raised heavenwards with the assistance of a pillar. It also included the small pyramids which were placed in niches in the tombs of Abydos or Deir el-Medina, and also the so-called "portable" or "micro-pyramids" which have occasionally been discovered. The identity of forms implies an identity of function; it suggests a magical flowing-down of celestial solar energy towards the earth. This double function is precisely the function which the ancient cosmogonies assigned to the central axis. The identity is confirmed by the rigorous orientation of the pyramids, the care which was taken in their construction, and their mathematical proportions.

These considerations surely enable us to suppose that the pyramids were monuments raised for a definite purpose. They are essentially artificial mountains, and, in accordance with ancient theories of the universe, they are able at one and the same time to serve as mountain-tombs of a solar character and as axial mountains situated at the centre of the universe or magically projected from it in a sacred geometrical form. They enclose within their foundations or walls, inside what may be termed artificial caves, the tombs of deified Pharaohs. At the precise point in space where they are situated, there is a break between the cosmic levels, a break that forms an inter-communication with the superior regions; and it was therefore here and nowhere else that the final metamorphosis of the royal Ka had the best chance of taking place. The function of the royal tomb was thus not a cause, but actually a consequence of the pyramidal form of architecture. It was also at the site of the royal tomb that, thanks to the adoption of the same pyramidal form, the flux of divine solar Energy spread in a spiritual and material manner over the whole length of Egypt.

If this interpretation is correct in general outline, it disposes of the old-fashioned idea that the pyramids were symbols of implacable pride, erected in the blood and sweat of an entire people. The author of this idea appears to have been Herodotus, a notoriously fanciful historian. His mistaken notion was due to the inability of the Greeks, and of subsequent generations, to understand the real motive of the Egyptians in building monuments of this kind. The pyramids were works of faith, raised not for the benefit of an individual Pharaoh (the notion of the "individual" is a peculiarly modern one), but for the benefit of the entire nation. The nation was literally incarnated in its King-God; it partook of the celestial privileges of his person, which was simultaneously divine and human. We have now travelled so far from philosophical concepts of this nature, that we can only grasp them as a result of the most strenuous intellectual effort; but we should realize that at one time they had the force of law, that they held sway over huge groups of human beings, and that the universe itself was incomprehensible without them.

None the less, we may hazard a guess that the Ancient Egyptians erected their pyramids for a reason which was not so very different from the reason for which modern engineers build dams, and modern scientists explore the universe of the atom. For, in covering the face of Egypt with pyramids, the Egyptians were trying to multiply the number of points of contact between the soil on which they trod and the heavens above them; they were attempting to call down upon the earth inexhaustible supplies of Energy.

The vast size of the pyramids, and the tremendous effort which must have gone into their construction, make a vivid contrast with the rudimentary techniques of building which, according to Egyptologists, must have been employed. These techniques have been the subject of much eager speculation. Two rival theories have usually been put forward as to the means which were employed. The first, following the account given by Herodotus, concerns itself with a number of liftingdevices, rough cranes operated by a human counterpoise. Cranes of this type, which could lift no more than a single block, would have had to be dismantled and remounted for every single layer of stone. There is no need to dwell on the complexity, slowness, and general inadequacy of such a system. The second theory, which postulates a series of swinging platforms raised from one layer to the next by means of wedges, is no better. The platforms would be stronger, but equally slow, equally overelaborate and equally exhausting to work.

Modern students have therefore put forward a fresh hypothesis, which makes use of a number of ramps. These ramps were supposed to have been huge in scale and were constructed of unfired bricks. The ramps were placed against the sides of the pyramids under construction, and raised simultaneously with the raising of the monument. Now, it is by no means unlikely that ramps of this sort were actually employed in the building of temples, where the walls were seldom more than thirty feet high. Remains of what may be such ramps have been discovered in the neighbourhood of certain temples. But there are serious difficulties when one attempts to attribute the use of ramps to the building of pyramids. In the first place, the erection of ramps a hundred feet high and a hundred feet long would have necessitated the most tremendous outlay of effort. Secondly, it is hard to see how ramps of crude brick could have been raised on a soil as unstable as that of Egypt. They would have been subject to the impossible wear-and-tear imposed on them by the continual comings and goings of men and materials. Ramps of one hundred feet or more in height would have required an inordinate amount of buttressing. Even so, they would have been subject to incessant bulging, breaking, and collapsing. The hoisting of great blocks of stone on to these ramps would have been an infinitely slow and laborious process. In conclusion, one would expect to find at least the vestiges of these accessory ramps, in the form of piles of debris, at a short distance from the surviving pyramid. Such vestiges have never been found, and this hypothesis would appear, in short, to be untenable.

Although it may seem somewhat foolhardy, we would like to put forward a third hypothesis which has not hitherto, so far as we know, been formulated. It certainly possesses more points in its favour than the two theories just mentioned. It has nothing to do with the construction of exterior ramps, and it therefore entails a considerable saving of time and effort. More, it disposes entirely with any human effort whatsoever in the lifting of the massive blocks, and it takes no account of frail or complex mechanisms of any sort. Finally, it would have enabled a considerable output of building materials.

The notion of ramps was retained by most authorities, despite the difficulties which it presents, because it was definitely utilized elsewhere in Egyptian architecture. But, one may ask, why was no account taken of the fact that the sides of the pyramid furnished a number of inclined planes, planes which took form during the course of the pyramid's construction? Of course, the slope of the sides was too steep to allow any sort of towing or hauling by means of human hands; but why may one not envisage the possibility of another kind of hauling? The men who furnished such striking testimony of engineering ability would surely have had the imagination to hit upon a very simple system of haulage. This was to build, on one or more sides of the pyramid under construction, either one or more series of parallel slides, on the stone-courses themselves. It should be borne in mind that at this stage the courses would not have been enclosed by their final dressing of white limestone. On the summit of the pyramid, on the platform made by the last completed course, would have been placed a huge drum (possibly made of wood, although wood was rare in Ancient Egypt), or a double drum revolving about the same axis. A cable wound round the drum would have enabled two sledges or platforms to have been raised or lowered. One of these platforms would have been up in the air when the other was down on the ground, and vice versa. Briefly, the idea resembles that of a primitive type of funicular, operated by means of counterpoises. The block which is to be raised is placed on the lower sledge and raised on one of the slides, while at the same time the other "bucket", filled with a counterweight, slides down to the bottom of the face of the pyramid. But what could this counter-weight be? It is quite clear that by making one inert mass go down to make another inert mass rise up, the builders would have been getting nowhere. A single satisfactory solution presents itself: the use of a *human* counterweight. In other words, the sides of the pyramid were the scene of frenzied and continuous activity, as gangs of men crowded on to the higher sledge in turn, keeping the whole operation in motion.

This hypothesis does not appear to run up against any insuperable technical or historical difficulty. Taking into account the average weight of, say, the Great Pyramid, and the loss of power due to friction and so forth, it seems reasonable to say that the weight of fifty workmen would have been sufficient to act as a counterpoise, in the way that we have briefly sketched out. There would naturally have been a number of important variants and improvements. The technique of the sledges would have been brought to a high point of empirical perfection by the Egyptians, in view of the formid-able weights which they had to shift; these weights were sometimes of the order of fifty tons or more. The manner of lashing the drums into position on top of the pyramids would not, surely, present an insoluble problem, although we are ignorant of the materials which might have been used to construct them and the kind of axis on which they turned.

The central idea of our hypothesis is that the Egyptians utilized what might be called the "power of weight" by a very simple and effective device. The ability to discover this device was not by any means beyond the genius of these prodigious movers of mountains.

At the present time, the traveller who looks around him can count a total of sixty man-made mountains on the soil of Egypt. Ceaselessly, in measure with the pacific rhythm of breeze and river, the royal barges sailed upstream and downstream to the great quarries of Tura, Gebel Silsileh and—far away in the south—Aswan. They sailed thither to seek huge blocks of limestone, sandstone or red granite; and these they hacked out, shaped and polished with mysterious perfection. Thousands of artisans worked on them, with the object of making the brute stone acceptable to the gods. As they worked, their sunburned heads shone beneath the pro-tecting fire of the true lord and master of Egypt, the Sun. And, one after the other, the gold-sheathed remains of the Pharaohs, children of Ra, departed into the deep shadows of stone and time to undergo the experi-ence of a supreme metamorphosis. Around that Form, whence flowed the solar power, were clustered innumerable cells, packed together like those in a beehive. Here lay an army of dead noblemen, lying with eyes wide open in their Houses-of-Eternity, whose walls were bedecked with frescoes that portrayed offerings, ships, harvests, harps, naked arms, reeds, smiles, and all those final gifts with which the living despatched the dead to their last home on the other side of things. Beyond, the common people huddled in geological strata, separated only by a few spadefuls of sand, eagerly taking in the last waves of the celestial flux.

33

Nothing, indeed, would appear to have been able to disturb an order of death as rigorous as that enclosed by these formidable walls. But even Egypt was unable to escape the mysterious law of oscillation to which the seas and peoples of the world are subject. And precisely because it succeeded in achieving such a high peak of accomplishment and certitude, the Old Kingdom came to know a corresponding agony of emptiness and internal collapse. Perhaps it was paying the price of a tension that had been too long prolonged. Something in its nature began to dissolve, to disintegrate; its foundations crumbled beneath the formidable weight of time, religious observance, and material prosperity. The first fissures appeared, then ran together like the filaments of a lightning flash. Insidiously they widened and became yawning breaches; and through them began to trickle streams of sand and chaos. There was a muddy, obscure period at the close of the Old Kingdom when the central power of the King-God declined, when it relapsed into a feudal brutality that oppressed the people. A layer of black ashes today records a great Egyptian upheaval, in which palaces and temples perished—three thousand seven hundred years before the torches of the French Revolution were kindled. A maddened crowd battered down the doors of the holy places, where for so long the secrets and treasures of the land had lain concealed. The mob plundered the bodies of the priests and nobles that lay there; it snatched hastily at the tiaras, the bracelets, the jewelled collars; it ran like a flame through the forbidden sanctuaries; it penetrated to the holy-of-holies of temples and burial-places and gazed insolently on the impassive faces of the hallowed dead. In the thick darkness, the victorious mob rummaged in search of hidden treasure and the secrets that bestowed immortality. And meanwhile, in the sunlit world outside, prostitutes were bedizening themselves in jewels and splendid raiment purloined for them by rapacious herdsmen. They spat on the ragged princesses who crouched on the dusty ground, dying of hunger. Potters ceased to make their pots, weavers to ply their shuttles, peasants to drive their wagons, artists to inscribe their dreams on stone. And at this critical moment, invaders whose eyes were cruel slits broke into the Delta, like a flock of vultures, and pillaged anything that

34

remained. The hurricane of Seth, the Destroyer, spirit of the storm and the red desert, descended on Egypt.

Yet, amid the wreckage, children continued to be born, the sun to shine, the river to carry down its soil. The wide scheme of things itself was untouched; and finally the Valley looked with compassion on its bewildered people. It murmured the immortal, healing words that could always be detected in the soft undertone of palms and reeds. Like gentle Isis, when she gathered up the bleeding remains of Osiris, the Valley restored to its people their former powers. Slowly, very slowly, the land began to smile again, its heart began once more to beat. At first this miraculous revival took place in the Delta. Then it reached Middle Egypt; and finally it progressed to the far south, to Thebes itself.

No other place was so characteristic of Ancient Egypt as Thebes. It lay beside the broad river—the slow, irresistible river, carrying towards the Delta the eddying mud, the trunks of trees, the reflections of birds of prey and of shoals of fish with flattened muzzles. To east and west were two narrow bands of fertile soil; and after a few miles the acid green of crops and date-palms gave place abruptly to sand, stones, and monumental cliffs of baked brown.

Thebes, the most perfect of all cities.
In the beginning, earth and water existed in it.
The sand was transformed into fertile soil
In order to create a place whence could rise the mound of the
    Creation of the World.
It was thus that the universe came into being.

Thebes drank always of the water of the river. And the modern Thebans closely resemble their predecessors, the Ancient Egyptians of the time of the Mentuheteps, the Amenemhats, the Sesostrises, and those other princes whose glorious names still produce an echo in the vault of history. In their day they were great princes, these Pharaohs of the Middle Kingdom, ruling from Thebes, who brought back unity to the Two Lands. They contained and ultimately drove out the Asian invader. They sent expedition after expedition to the fabulous regions of Sinai and Punt. They fertilized whole stretches of desert, and erected dams, reservoirs, and works of irrigation. They re-established justice, and brought the gods once more into repute.

A few pyramids of the Middle or New Kingdoms have been discovered in the neighbourhood of the Delta; but as examples of the art of pyramid-building there is no denying that they lack conviction. The pyramid of Deir el-Bahri was supported on four square porticoes, and was nothing more than a contrasting motif to the great natural pyramid that loomed behind it. This was the Mountain of the West, the abode of a goddess who was revered as the protectress of burial-places and "lover of silence". From the Middle Kingdom onwards, religious philosophy was to manifest itself in works of a less abstract kind. The people who thronged the outer court-yard were now able, thanks to the revolution, to take part in the rites which were celebrated in the depths of the sanctuary. The temples which sprung up anew, to reaffirm the link between the land of Egypt and the realm of the invisible, strike the modern spectator like huge organisms of stone tramping through the centuries, not like ephemeral edifices. Temples dedicated to similar purposes were built in India, Greece, and medieval Europe, but in these places the conception of the architect appears to be in some sense static. In the case of the Theban temples, however, it seems that a more transcendent habit of thought was at work, a habit of thought born from the dual contemplation of moving river and petrified horizon. It was compounded on one hand of an eternity of motion, on the other of an eternity of immobility. It combined the twin visages of the universe as they knew it, Energy, and the landscape of Egypt itself. By an odd paradox, Ancient Egypt is thus the civilization which, although to the first superficial glance it appears immobile, actually gave rise to the unique, staggering conception of an architecture of movement. In Egyptian architecture, Form was incarnate in the most intractable material. It was conceived, developed, renewed, flowered, died, by means of a mystic transformation of inert matter into a living entity. What screenwriter, even though carried in some Wellsian time-machine, could ever convey by high-speed or slow-motion film the successive blossomings, advances, retreats, contractions and amoebic proliferations of such a building as the Temple of Karnak?

The Temple of Karnak gives the impression of incompletion, of a work in perpetual motion. It was constantly undergoing alteration and aggrandizement. Every prince and every dynasty considered it an honour to add another court, another colossus, another pylon. The result is that the building is really an agglomeration of temples that are juxtaposed, superimposed, packed one on top of the other. Successive generations of builders systematically broke up the monuments of their predecessors; they shattered the statues of an earlier period into a thousand pieces, and hid the broken remnants in the earth. It was as though they wished to sow the seeds of the new building that would spring magically from the soil. But this new building was destined to be neither more perfect nor less perfect than its predecessor. It would contain the same stereotyped inscriptions, couched in the same stereotyped terms. To us, this kind of systematic annihilation and ritual murder is artistically completely unjustifiable. But surely it bears witness to a subtle, unswerving desire to perpetuate a view of life based on immutable certainties? Ancient Egypt had discovered the secret of shaping the future from the contemplation of the past.

Is it possible that Ancient Egypt had achieved an equilibrium that is unknown to ourselves? It had been liberated from the ties of the past, it was free from illusion about the morrow. It held in its hands the keys of its own destiny. Its apparent immobility stems from the fact that it escaped from the labyrinth of time. Incessantly it destroyed and repeated the same formulas, dramas, and divine images. But we must be careful when we say that it repeated them incessantly: for there was no taint of exhaustion about this repetition. Generation after generation of artists launched forth upon the exploration of the same forms, with a passion that was always fresh and a sense of marvel that was always new. Such a sense of renewal is almost miraculous in our own day and age, when every mediocre dauber pretends to be a unique individual, and a towering genius into the bargain. But in those immeasurably distant times of which we are speaking, art was essentially sacred, and thus collective in character. It sprang directly from an inexhaustible source. The repetition of the identical themes, imposed upon the artist by popular belief, did not serve in the least to make his imagination sterile. There was, in fact, no repetition in our modern sense of the term: that is to say, the boring reiteration of the same idea until it finally becomes trivial and unimportant. Where Ancient Egypt was concerned, one might as well accuse the sea of imitating the waves that follow each other towards the shore.

From the Middle Kingdom to the end of the New Kingdom, a period that lasted about a thousand years, a formidable effusion of energy flowed along the Valley, carrying everything before it. The only interruption was the short and brutal interregnum that followed an invasion of Asiatic peoples known as the Hyksôs. Along the whole stretch of the Nile, granite and basalt, limestone and sandstone were hacked out, perforated, sawn up, sculpted, polished, hauled from place to place, and erected with extraordinary ease and certainty. The blocks of stone were handled with a royal indifference to the technical difficulties involved. The way in which these difficulties were overcome is inexplicable, unless one realizes that what was involved was the element of faith, the faith that is able to move mountains.

Even this legendary faith, however, was subject to vacillations. At first the princes of the New Kingdom tended more and more towards a theocratic form of religion. Amon-Ra, the All-Powerful, the Hidden One, ruled with increasing absolutism over Thebes and over the destinies of the Empire. At this critical juncture, there arose in the land one of the most enigmatic figures known to history. This was the Pharaoh Amenophis IV of the Eighteenth Dynasty, the monarch with an intriguing, sickly face, the famous "heretic king". He was the son of Amenophis III, the builder of Luxor, and in his early days he was particularly devoted to Amon-Ra, in

38

whose religion he had been carefully nurtured. At length, however, for some unknown reason he began to engage in desperate strife with the god of Thebes, and ultimately dispersed his clergy and caused his image to be hammered out of the monuments. He even went so far as to change his own name from Amenophis to Akhenaton. But the spirit of Amon-Ra had thoroughly impregnated the city of Thebes, and soon Pharaoh ran into inevitable difficulties. In a storm of passion, he shook the dust of Thebes from off his sandals, and he set out to found a new administrative and religious capital on virgin soil. This capital was the city of Tel el-Amarna, and the only god worshipped within its precincts was the sun-god Aton, the solar disc. Aton was not wholly an innovation of Akhenaton, but an aspect of Amon-Ra which had been previously honoured at Heliopolis, a rival religious centre to Thebes. When he took the name *Akhenaton* in place of his own patronymic, Pharaoh was calling himself "Glory of the Aton".

Certain persons have tried to elevate Akhenaton to the position of herald of monotheism, a great religious reformer, even an early forerunner of Christianity. This interpretation is somewhat hazardous, and would appear to be contradicted by certain salient facts. In the first place, if we are to believe that Akhenaton was the apostle of monotheism, we would have to be certain that the religion of Amon-Ra, which he overthrew, was truly polytheistic. This cannot be proved, and such a polytheism would be in contradiction to the synthesizing tendency which is the hallmark of Ancient Egyptian civilization: the innumerable divinities worshipped by the Egyptians appear to have coalesced into a single unique and transcendental expression of godlike energy. One should beware of regarding the innumerable sacred relics and images that one finds scattered throughout the length and breadth of Egypt as incontrovertible evidence of polytheism. The archaeologists of the future would be equally at fault if they were to infer the existence of a multiplicity of cults from the innumerable statues of the saints which are associated with Christianity.

It has often been said that the stigmata of mysticism and reforming zeal can be seen stamped upon the sculpted features of Akhenaton. Even this is open to question. May not the monarch's features be redolent, rather, of voluptuousness and sensuality? It is a matter of personal interpretation. In any case, to substitute for the abstract cult of Amon-Ra, as it was consummated in the dim shrines of his temples, the cult of a solar-disc, and to celebrate the cult of the disc in the open air before the gaze of all, was surely to proceed towards a materialistic rather than idealistic conception of the Divine Being. Again, the art which flourished at Tel el-Amarna was not in the least hieratic in style; on the contrary, it was realistic and often descended to caricature.

It is reasonable to suppose that Akhenaton was above all a poet, a poet of Nature. The statues of him that survive show beyond doubt that he was an invalid; but he was also a man possessed of high inspiration. There is inspiration in every line of his famous *Hymn to the Sun*, whose tone evokes a tender and delicate love of the living universe. Why, one wonders, did he find it necessary to leave Thebes? He never appears to have been in any degree a politically-minded person. Was it some form of revolt against his father? Or was it a personal antipathy towards the High Priest of Amon-Ra? This animosity might have been engendered in a highly individual, anarchic personality by the hostility of a religious order that depended in its very nature upon rigid conformity. But whatever the reason, it is perfectly evident that Pharaoh's so-called reforms were ephemeral. His vaunted new capital lasted only a few years and was quickly deserted. After only fifty years, it was abandoned to the desert, to the cobras and the pitiless winds. The Pharaoh's cartouches and stelae were desecrated in their turn, and nothing remained of this extraordinary spiritual venture than a few fragmentary inscriptions and artistic images. Some of these incompleted artistic achievements are careless, even scurrilous in character, but some of them are carried out with the most ravishing sense of spontaneity. Above all, the Amarna period has bequeathed to us one object of universal admiration: the renowned head of Queen Nefertiti, grave and spiritual, informed with overwhelming humanity. . . .

Amon-Ra had triumphed. Once again the old battle between Egypt and the scale of Nature was renewed. This time it was couched primarily in the form of tremendous buildings, in which man tried by means of prodigious efforts to inject his own breathing soul. It was at this period that Karnak was built. Here, beyond the second pylon, one is plunged into the shadow and silence of a remarkable forest. It is a forest of stone, in which a hundred and thirty-four giant tree-trunks, their bases silted by the sand, provide a refuge for birds and for the gods. The rays of the sun can hardly penetrate the stone foliage of this temple, which was built by Ramses II. It was this mighty Pharaoh who made additions to the handi-work of Amenophis III at Luxor. (One of the obelisks which he erected there now discharges its solar arrow into the Parisian sky.) Later, Ramses hewed a tremendous temple from the sheer cliffs of Abu Simbel, five hundred miles south of Thebes. The temple is shot through with cosmic grandeur, and it is impossible to distinguish the work of man from the work of Nature. What appears to be the spur of the cliff turns out, on closer inspection, to be the shapely limb of a god; and what looks like the torso of a god is discovered to be a jutting portion of the cliff. No Pharaoh constructed his buildings with an eye on eternity with more assurance than the mighty Ramses. The frieze of cynocephalous deities that crowns the ramparts of Abu Simbel still continues, three thousand two hundred years afterwards, to greet the shining face of Ra as it appears each morning above the rim of the lower world.

But although the Ancient Egyptians were obsessed by the sun, their imagination was always haunted by the shadows. They went in awe of the shadows of the night and the shadows of death. These were the shadows which crept towards them every sunset from the great mountain of the east, sliding insidiously into the valley, spreading like lava, inching across the river, insinuating themselves into the temples and dwelling-places of Thebes.

In Egypt, two worlds were face to face: the world of the living and the world of the dead, separated only by the great barrier of the Nile. The very structure of the country lent itself to contrasting symbols whose meaning was apparent to even the humblest intellect. The idea of a last voyage across a river is known to other mythologies; we find it, for example, in the *Divina Commedia*. But perhaps the innermost mystery of Egyptian civilization is to be found in this correlation between metaphor and brute fact, between ideas suggested by the appearance of the landscape and ideas stemming purely from the imagination.

The courtiers, the priests, the Pharaohs, the rich and poor—one after the other they entered the shades, amid the flicker of torchlight, the cries of the mourners lining the banks of the river. They knew that this was their common fate. But they knew also that a redeeming pathway could be found to lead them through the mazes of the Other World. The goddess Isis had discovered how to persuade the secret gates of the underworld to open for her lord Osiris. She had accomplished her task with the aid of magic, of love, and of the mysterious spirit of helpfulness that pervades the universe. The dead of Ancient Egypt, huddled in their tombs, were in the same sad predicament as Isis. Like her, they were seeking to find and to pronounce the Master Words which alone would bring salvation. No other people made such strenuous efforts—physical, intellectual, artistic, financial—to ensure for its dead a happy survival. No other people gave such evidence of a feeling of human fellowship extending beyond the tyranny of time. One can contrast, without irony, the phrases about "eternal loving memory" written on modern tombstones. This "memory" is fortunate if it lasts for a single century.

Ancient Egypt, denying death, discovered on the horizon itself the landscape of eternity. In order to escape from annihilation, it was necessary to make use of enduring stone, the only material that was capable of protecting the dead from external molestation. Stone was living, like everything else in the universe. It was stone which would enable the dead man to achieve his proper death. Crowds of workmen would erect above his head his House of Millions of Years, which would ensure that another sun would infuse its energy into the sleeper. The purpose of this process of petrifaction was to immobilize the dead person in a superhuman dimension where the relative motions of space and time would cease to exist. Materially, the process would be brought about by following the immortalizing precepts of mummification; and afterwards the body was inhumed in a

42

cavern drilled in the solid rock. At Thebes, this inhumation took place in the bowels of the natural mountain-pyramid, the Mountain of the West.

In the tomb there took place the mystical crossing of the river from east to west. For the more privileged classes of society, there was also a funerary pilgrimage to the sacred shrine of Abydos, a holy place where the tomb of Osiris, the God of Resurrection, was originally supposed to have been located.

At last the body was laid away in its final resting-place. It was swathed in a robe, masked, embalmed and perfumed, covered with talismans and protective images, enveloped in the voluminous bandages that transformed it into a giant cocoon. It was now ready to submit to the mysterious alchemy of metamorphosis. For the illustrious man, one coffin was not enough. He was encased in one coffin after another, like Chinese boxes. Each coffin was lavishly ornamented with tiny signs and pictures, incorporating the most efficacious magical formulas; and these coffins in their turn were housed within a weighty sarcophagus, which itself was enclosed inside as many as four shrines, fitting one inside the other. This strange dead fruit, in its multiple protecting shells, was hidden away a hundred yards from the sunlight, in the deepest of a series of fantastic artificial caverns. The caverns were hewn out of the virgin rock, with a titanic effort whose scope was known to the gods alone. The most ambitious tombs of Egypt are labyrinths, laboriously sealed with triple portcullises of granite. They contain vertical pits and shafts, and are full of concealed traps and tricks. The shafts and galleries have often been filled up in order to disguise their presence. It is safe to say that no similar barricades between the living and the dead have been thrown up in any other part of the world.

In the case of the larger tombs, these barriers were erected for reasons of State. As in the pyramids, the protection of the remains of a dead Pharaoh was a national necessity. The whole people was associated with his divine death. Not only for his own repose and peace of spirit, but also for those of his people, it was necessary that Pharaoh should thread his way successfully through the innumerable ambuscades of Hades. The Underworld was a

43

kind of mirror in which the world of the living was reflected in an inverted manner. Through it ran a river Nile; but it was a funereal Nile, on which silently glided, during the hours of the night, the ghostly boats that carried the shadowy forms of the gods. There on the river, and upon its banks, lurked the dim forms with which the instinctive poetry of the Ancient Egyptians had peopled them. We may repeat that the extraordinary precautions taken by the priests to seal and reseal the great royal tombs were primarily intended to foil the attempts of robbers, attracted by the lure of buried treasure. As a secondary consideration, it was also necessary to raise obstacles to keep at bay the evil and incorporeal forces which were ever on the prowl.

Whatever their intention, their precautions were useless. Everything that man has been able to build, man has also been able to destroy. The sacred tombs were violated, and they were violated in antiquity. One of the paradoxes of Egyptian history is that, at a time when men were moved by faith to build elaborate temples and even more elaborate burial-places, there were also men who were sufficiently bold and covetous to break into them. They willingly defied the magical rules that were everywhere in operation, and this at a time when the prestige of magic must have been very high. The robbers triumphed over the watchfulness of the appointed guardians of the great cemeteries, perhaps with the aid of counter-charms fashioned in the darkness by some wizard. In their ability to surmount the formidable obstacles designed to keep them out, they showed a skill as remarkable as that of the architects. And at last they broke through and laid sacrilegeous hands on the riches crammed within the burial chamber itself. Sometimes, as later law-cases show, they undertook their raids with the collaboration of corrupt keepers of the cemetery, or of renegade priests.

These robberies took place so frequently that the priests of Thebes were forced to adopt a desperate remedy—desperate, that is, in relation to ancient tradition. They were compelled to take the royal mummies from their tombs and re-inter them with the greatest secrecy in a carefully-chosen hiding-place. They did their work so well that it was only in 1881 that their hiding-place was discovered, not far from Deir el-Bahri. The

44

frightful disorder in which it was found revealed the haste with which this clandestine operation, involving thirteen royal mummies and the bodies of several princes and princesses, had been carried out.

But if all the gold and silver formerly placed in Egyptian tombs has been dispersed, in museums and collections throughout the world, there still remains within the grand cavern of the Valley of the Kings a treasure of whose value the ancient robbers were not cognizant. This treasure is the series of frescoes which give life to the tomb-walls, creating there a stupendous funeral ballet. Here, despite the disarray of the empty rooms and gutted sepulchres, a measure of ancient magic still persists. The sight of these pictures, pure and peaceful or contorted and monstrous, still awakens strange echoes. One realizes yet again that if this ancient art appears unreal, its unreality is not in the least accidental. Western painting, driven out of its classical position by machines which are capable of making endless reproductions of an original image, has been searching during the last few decades for a refuge on the harsh summits of "abstraction". In its search, it has been rediscovering a mode of expression lost to it since before the Renaissance. But only too often, because many Western artists are in two minds about the god or devil to whom they should pay their homage, our art has been lost in sterile deserts of artificial construction which make no profound or personal appeal to anyone, beyond the superficial appeal of pleasing colours. Our art has tended to lie on the surface of the canvas. In contrast, the cultivation of what may be called genuine irrealism is not at all arbitrary, and takes no account of intellectual traits. It is the art of Hieronymus Bosch, of the tympanum of twelfth-century cathedrals, of Theban tomb-painting. It is an art which is founded with complete logic on a substratum of sacred belief. It expresses the fantasia of the unconscious, projected into a world of material appearances. It gives form to the perma-nent and authentic manifestations of the psyche. And this forgotten artistic language is still capable of producing a quiver in our breasts.

We do not know the precise meaning intended to be conveyed by the frescoes of Ancient Egypt. Experts tell us that they are illustrations to such literary works as the *Book of Gates*, the *Hymns to the Sun*, the *Book of*

Opening-the-Mouth and the *Book of What-is-in-the-Underworld*. This is no doubt true; but since the paintings stand for suggestions and symbols, we can never know what these artistic images truly and accurately represent. Because of this, the impression which they convey is bound to be somewhat enfeebled; but it is nevertheless true that they pierce our minds like arrows.

The mural art of Egypt produces a remarkable sense of completeness. Not only has it something of definite character to say, but it is also full of purely plastic fascination. It is extraordinary that the orthodox histories of art should have practically ignored this school of painting. There is a whole Louvre of great mural-paintings at Thebes. It is only necessary to instance the gallery of Seti I, the tombs of Ramses III, Tuthmosis and Horemhab. Each of these tombs contains important variations of style and composition. The walls glimmer in the semi-darkness with gold and pale red, with lapis lazuli and delicate yellow. On them is depicted a fantastic procession of figures from the living world and from the Underworld, animated by a bold and inexhaustible creative imagination.

The Egyptian capacity for design, demonstrated by a remarkable ability to synthesize, is everywhere subordinated to the ruling conventions of Egyptian art. This art is essentially based on the magical interpretation of images. It takes no account of the "laws of perspective", though it is quite evident that the painters of these masterpieces would certainly have been able to make use of *trompe-l'œil* if they had wanted to. No, these works ignore perspective because they were not intended to reproduce the mere physical appearance of things. Their function was strictly bound up with myth and belief. In the sombre galleries of Theban tombs, as well as on the sunlit faces of the great temple-pylons, the artist was not concerned with reproducing things that he actually saw, but things that existed in his mind. He thought of these things in all their spatial totality. What he considered important was the presentation of things in their synthetic aspect, in a manner at once subtle and condensed. He thus projected different aspects of his subject simultaneously, in the same work and in the same plane. That is why figures in Egyptian art have their legs in profile, their bodies turned to the front, their heads twisted sideways, their eyes full-face. The way in which they are represented is thus unreal from a strictly ocular point of view; but it certainly presents what might be called a "total" image of the person depicted, irrespective of the conventions of space and time. It therefore attempts to achieve a kind of super-resemblance; and this super-resemblance, by means of an ancient theory of sympathetic magic, is capable of becoming the person himself.

Every effort was made to preserve the material integrity of the form concerned. As the pursuit of perspective would entail its mutilation, perspective was omitted by Egyptian artists. As for composition, it was conceived in vertical and horizontal planes, treated rather in the manner of a map. The same fundamental principle governed the way in which the paint was laid on in flat washes.

The handling of a conventional repertoire was not an artistic phenomenon common to Ancient Egypt alone, but appears to belong to a certain universal state of religious thought. However that may be, inside these conventions the Egyptian artist wrought miracles. It is a sad error on the part of an artist to claim a total "liberty" for his art, also a complete absence of rules. Such so-called liberty often results in a kind of plastic and intellectual dissolution of the work in hand. Many compositions or pieces of sculpture that are labelled "progressive" often remind one of unformed chaos. They are a flat contradiction of the meaning of art, for art consists in giving recognizable shape to inert matter. On the contrary, the more rules that are imposed on the artist, the more the completed work will gain in power and intrinsic energy: provided, of course, that the rules are well-defined and that the artist accepts them. In the measure in which creative genius is poured out in relative forms, by so much it aspires to universality. This is particularly so with artistic forms created during those epochs which are called archaic. The apparent weaknesses of the art of these periods only serve, in the final analysis, to strengthen the profound impression which they make on the mind, often against all logic.

It is entirely useless to attempt to compare the works of art of Ancient Egypt with those created in the Western world since the Renaissance, and since the so-called "discovery" of the laws of perspective. It is equally foolish to express a preference for either the ancient or the modern modes of expression. Beginning with a certain set of conventions (and perspective itself is only a convention), every artistic style is developed according to its own rules. It describes a complete cycle and furnishes its own particular masterpieces. The only valid individual preference is that which is based on a knowledge of psychology, and on the realization that such a preference is bound to be relative. The whole difference between the great mural paintings of Thebes and, say, the frescoes of Michelangelo in the Sistine Chapel, is that the first were intended to ornament a space of a sacred nature, the second to decorate a room, even though that room happened to be in a chapel. Sometimes it happens that a genius is born who brings to his work a sense of the magic of a former age; and that is why certain passages in the work of Michelangelo, such as the "Creation of Adam" or the portrait of Moses, are bathed, despite the fact that they belong to a different age and are carried out by different technical means, in an atmosphere of primitive magic.

The walls of the royal tombs bring before us a unique cortège of innumerable scenes and figures from a religious epoch that resembles the Christian Middle Ages. The mortuary-temples of the same princes, connected with their tombs by passages hewn through the solid mass of the mountain, bring before our gaze a completely different pictorial repertoire. The interior of the temples are decorated with the customary religious themes, but the surfaces of the pylons outside are scored with monumental bas-reliefs depicting the great events of the reigns of individual monarchs, preserving their deeds for posterity. On these huge expanses of stone, the sculptors have engraved compositions whose breadth of conception is on the same regal scale as the subjects with which they deal. The reliefs are perfectly suited to the architectural form of the pylons; but despite their great size they still find a place for the most remarkable abundance of detail. These reliefs are like film epics where, amid a great throng of extras, the superhuman figure of Pharaoh rises like a giant among pygmies. He sits upon his throne, or he rides out to the chase or the field of battle, carried forward by beautifully caparisoned steeds whose flying legs are fixed for ever in the cold stone. He is always young, always handsome, always triumphant. He is the idealized projection of the people in whom he is incarnate, and which recognizes itself in him. Sometimes the stone seems literally to flicker, to pant for breath—such is the intensity of the artist's inspiration. In the great mural sculptures of the Ramasseum one can see, and almost hear, the clash of arms, the collapse of scaling-ladders, the shrieks of the dying. Chariots hurtle forward; masses of men break and flee; prisoners flatten themselves on the ground, imploring the mercy of the victorious Pharaoh; or else, clasped by hydra-headed monsters with a hundred arms, like the arms of Kali in Indian art, they await the final brutal blow of the axe. At the palace-temple of Medinet Habu, one can view the great hunt of Ramses III. Here, in a magnificent composition, informed with a quasi-musical rhythm, we can see the flight of fear-crazed antelopes. We can admire the powerful outlines of bull-like creatures, perishing beneath the arrows of their pursuers, dropping down with their muzzles in the oozy slime of the marshes. Elsewhere are graven frescoes that depict the fortunes of other battles, the fate of other captives.

The walls of the temple of Hatshepsut relate a whole series of stories; or, rather, they whisper them, for the reliefs and paintings are silted in the wastes of sand. On the walls are recorded the fabulous achievements of ancient expeditions to the land of Punt, which may be modern Somaliland. The stately ships of the Queen sail upon the broad ocean; the captain stands upon the bridge, in conversation with the pilot. And in other panels are shown the subjugated tribes, the exchange of gifts of incense and antimony, gold and ivory. We are shown the jungle, and the wild men who inhabited it. These wild creatures were later captured and brought back to Egypt, to provide a spectacle for the Queen and her courtiers.

The tumultuous tales of glory and adventure on the walls of royal tombs and temples subside rapidly when we find ourselves in the tombs of civilians. These are the humbler tombs that were huddled against each other on the eastern flank of the cliff. In these civilian tombs the artists specialized in portraying the whole daily life of Ancient Egypt. They portrayed it in such a way that it flourished with wonderful freshness and purity even in the shadowy darkness, where it seemed to take away the sting and the reproach of death. The painted frescoes in these tombs assure us that the sunlit gaiety of a race who, after all, were the children of the sun, succeeded in vanquishing eternal night. Thirty-two centuries after the artist's brush delineated it upon the walls, a happy crowd of people continues to go about its daily task. The washerwomen continue to launder; peasants continue to till the land and harvest their crops; sailors continue to put out to sea; scribes continue to draw up their accounts. The subjects of the frescoes are shown in the hunting-field, or at their dinner-table. They listen to music, take part in processions, quarrel, make love, weep, and laugh. Above all they laugh, always they laugh. They are a smiling, light-hearted people, these inhabitants of the shades. On their faces is the secret, slightly melancholy smile that can still be seen on the face of the young fellah who goes down to the river in the twilight to water his buffalo. It is the smile of a people that has run the whole gamut of experience, a people who have known defeat and glory, who have lived, loved, suffered, created, and destroyed. It is the smile of an ancient race which ceased long ago to be duped by itself or others, and still remembers with a vague pride its old grandeur and its erstwhile gods.

Night has fallen on the Valley, and on the Great Mountain of Thebes. Thirty centuries ago the New Empire reached its apogee under the great Ramses, and was acclaimed by standards flapping from poles of pylons and the strident ring of copper trumpets. The wind appeared to be set fair for an eternity of Egyptian national glory. And then—slowly—the clock seemed to unwind and run down. In the course of a millennium, Ancient Egypt foundered with majestic slowness. The ambitions of the high priests of Thebes undermined the authority of the last Theban Ramessides. The vital unity of the nation burst asunder; the country found itself delivered over increasingly to sordid political manœuvres, to the petty rivalry of local dynasts. In east, west, and south, the colonial grip of Egypt relaxed. The conquered peoples of the Empire, whether Asiatic or Syrian, Libyan or Nubian, seized their opportunity to escape from the grasp of the Egyptian. The building of temples still continued; but all the time the

50

pitiless robbers were pillaging the royal burial places. Then, one after another, waves of invaders fanned out across the ancient landscape, a landscape that Amon had ceased to defend. The waves retired, then flowed back once more, shaking the very foundations of a State already divided against itself. The Double Crown of the Pharaohs toppled and fell to the earth, the vulture became locked in a death struggle with the Uraeus. Eventually, as a final indignity, an Ethiopian mounted the throne of Egypt. And next, without warning, the Assyrian army ground its way like a steamroller as far as Thebes. And then came the Libyans, the Persians, the Greeks, the Romans.

Egypt defended itself badly. It was as though a secret wound had opened in some portion of the great inert body, releasing the blood drop by drop. By breaking the royal seals on the tombs of the Pharaohs, by defying the beliefs which protected the royal remains, the tomb robbers had accomplished a symbolic, decisive gesture. They had liberated their country from the ancient spells which held it together. But it was to these very spells that the Ancient Egyptians owed the fact that they were able continually to rise above themselves, to set out ceaselessly on a high adventure that had no other aim than the conquest of immortality. And at the same time the robbers had loosed other forces. They had set free the malignant Seth, enemy of the sun, lord of destruction and darkness. The old order had been reduced, owing to the furbishing of centuries, to the fragility of crystal. It had been built up with such fine grained logic that a single crack would imperil the entire structure.

Egypt was overcome by the same malady that afflicted all the old high civilizations. This was the malady of indifference, the price that had to be paid for the wisdom which they achieved. The Egyptians had experienced so much that they were unable to see a single point of view, but were always forced to take account of every side of every question. They had become so subtle minded that they were unable to resist the temptation to carry every dogma to its logical conclusion.

So Egypt itself had arrived before the Gate of Night. The inescapable Law which had impelled everything towards the Mountain of Silence, the sun as well as man, finally affected the civilization of which they formed part. Any resistance to such a destiny would have been a useless insult to the gods. The time had come for Egypt to lie down meekly in the funeral-boat and sail across the River. Ancient Egypt had outlived its faith; and it was dead.

But it took ten centuries to die. The gods still loomed above the chaos and the delirium of the time—nailed to their cliffs, towering on the walls of their great sanctuaries. The barbarian and the iconoclastic Persian tried vainly to mutilate the noble figures whose calm defiance they could not stomach. Vainly they tried to humiliate the soul of a race whose dignity infuriated them. Sweating and panting, they pulled down the sacred buildings in an attempt to create a death-bed for the gods on the wreck of their temples. But the ravaged head that rolled on the ground in front of them still mocked them with its invincible smile. Each new injury caused the mysterious efficacy of the gods to grow.

Successive generations of artists still continued to recreate with unabated energy the old hieratic forms. Yet more and more they turned their faces towards a past that had really and truly become "the past". The Greeks, with their keen intelligence, came later to appreciate the moral grandeur which they found in Egypt, and they sought to reanimate its pristine religious fires. The Greek temples of Kom Ombo, Dendera and Edfu, which took two hundred years of backbreaking effort to build, are the ultimate limits of Egyptian aspiration. In these temples the head of the serpent has begun to eat the tail, and the complete cycle was finally brought to an end in a sumptuous architectural efflorescence worthy of the architecture that had preceded it. But then the living breath itself died away. . . .

Thus came to an end one of the most astonishing spiritual adventures the world has ever seen. The long wake on the ocean of time faded from sight. We enlightened folk of the twentieth century are reduced to timid silence by the relics of this perished civilization. Despite all our culture, and despite our naïve assumption of superiority, we can only stand and stare. No book, film, or photograph can explain the strange glamour we feel when confronted by these stupendous remains. They pose, moreover, a number of questions which arise from our modern habits of thought, our idiosyncratic customs, our peculiar conception of the universe. According to the new mythology, and to the factors which we believe govern the course of history, the activities of the Ancient Egyptians do not correspond with what we recognize as "reality". What, we ask, were the use of these frantic, fantastic labours on behalf of imaginary divinities? What were the use of these temples, colossi, hypogeums, pyramids? What was the use of this persistence in the face of constant destruction? What were the use of these colossal efforts which swallowed up so much strength and treasure, so much intelligence and sweat? Does not the true drama of Ancient Egypt reside, we ask ourselves, in the fact that the ends which it pursued so doggedly were really non-existent?

It is not difficult to find an answer to these questions. The answer will depend, of course, on the extent to which we are personally capable of attaining a relative point of view. Surely, if we look at things *sub specie aeternitatis,* the formidable amount of energy expended by the Ancient Christians was not expended in vain? Surely it is only by hurling himself against the hard shell of the universe that man is able, in the course of a long process of trial and error, to discover his true nature and realize his essential humanity. No people ever devoted themselves more courageously to the conquest of time and matter than the people of Ancient Egypt. Their whole history is an obstinate attempt to outstrip their own considerable achievements. They played, in their time and place, an essential part in the evolution of the human species. We would not have been what we are if the Ancient Egyptians had not been what they were.

In conclusion, then, that which we call "reality" is a purely relative idea. Each epoch redefines reality according to its own conception, which is usually completely opposed to the conceptions that went before. The ideas which informed Ancient Egypt and gave it its unique character may seem erroneous to us in the middle of the twentieth century. But, in their own time, these ideas were just as "true" as those in which we believe today. They were just as effective or impotent as our own ideas will seem to the generations ahead. One should remember the words of Saint-Exupéry: "What is important for a man is that which makes him a man." Similarly, what counts for a mob is that which makes it a people. It does not matter what paths men choose if they lead eventually to the high peaks. And it was these high peaks that the great ones of Egypt attained. The works of art which they have left behind are irrefutable evidence of this.

Their temples have crumbled. Their colossi are broken. The seals of their burial-places are cracked asunder. Their bodies, which they prepared with such elaborate art for the long voyage to the next world, have returned to dust. The natron, the bandages, the triple sarcophagus . . . these have availed them nothing. . . .

But from any one of those mutilated, god-like faces, from those sight-less eyes, from those lips that will open never more, springs a triple barb of gold, launched with the full power of the sun. And this barb brings with it a message which has pierced space, time, and the barriers of Cartesianism. It is a message that brings us wisdom, and beauty, and silence.

SAMIVEL

PLATES

I.

LA VALLÉE
THE VALLEY

2.
LE DELTA
THE DELTA

3.
FAYOÛM
THE FAYÛM

4.
ASSOUAN....
ASWAN....

5.
...ET SES DÉSERTS
...AND THE SURROUNDING DESERT

6.
LA FIN DU MONDE
THE END OF THE WORLD

7.

LA MONTAGNE DES DIX COMMANDEMENTS
THE HILL OF THE TEN COMMANDMENTS

8.

LES ALPES DE GIZEH ——►
THE MOUNTAINS OF GIZA

The Wisdom of Ptahhotep

Do not let your heart become proud because of what you know;
Learn from the ignorant as well as from the learned man.
There are no limits that have been decreed for art;
There is no artist who attains entire excellence.

A lovely thought is harder to come by than a jewel;
One can find it in the hand of a maid at the grindstone.

Do not let your heart become swollen with pride
In case it may be humbled.

It is true that one may become rich through doing evil,
But the power of Truth and Justice is that they endure
And that a man can say of them: "They are a heritage from my father."

If you are resolute, acquire a reputation
For knowledge and kindliness.

Follow the dictates of your heart.

Let your face shine during the time that you live . . .
It is the kindliness of a man that is remembered
During the years that follow . . .

Fifth Dynasty, c. 2500 B.C.

The Wisdom of the Pharaoh Kheti

The Judges who give judgment on the downtrodden,
You know how rigorous they are
When the day dawns for judging the guilty,
When the momentous hour arrives!

Woe results when the prosecutor is the Wise One;
Put not your trust in longevity.
Where these judges are concerned, a lifetime lasts but a single hour.
Man survives death,
And a man's actions are heaped at his side.
One is faced with the prospect of eternity;
The person who makes light of it is an idiot!

But the man who comes stainless before his judges
Abides in the hereafter like a god,
Marching proudly forward
Like those who possess the keys of eternity.

Be not ruthless, for it is fine to be generous;
Act in such a way that your work will endure because it is endearing.
Speak the truth in your house
So that the great ones who rule the land will hold you in respect . . .
It is the inside of the house that compels outward admiration.

Do not exalt someone of noble birth
More than you do the child of a humble man,
But choose a man because of his actions.

The virtue of a man whose heart is just is more acceptable to God
Than the choice bull of the man who commits iniquity.

c. 2070 B.C.

The Wisdom of Any

Where God is, uproar is abhorred.

Pray with a loving heart
In which the loving words are all enfolded.

When you are a young man,
When you take a wife and set up house,
Remember how your mother brought you into the world
And with what embracing care she nurtured you.
Never give her cause to accuse you
And lift up her hands towards God in condemnation of your conduct,
And never give God reason to listen to your mother's complaints!

Do not let your conduct in the household be too high-and-mighty,
And never lord it over your wife, if you know that she
    is a gentle-hearted woman.
Do not say to her: "Where is so and so? Bring it here!"
When she has put it away carefully in some safe place.
Keep her beneath your eye and watch her silently
In appreciation of her worth.
She is contented when your hand rests upon hers.

c. 1300 B.C.

69

The Wisdom of Amenemope

The man who respects the poor is beloved of God.

Be not covetous of wealth.
You can swallow down a fat morsel,
But you may vomit it up,
And be emptier than you were before . . .
Better a single bushel bestowed by God
Than five thousand ill-gotten . . .
When you hear things spoken of that are of good or evil report,
Reject the latter, as though it had never come to your ears.
Keep a sweet word ever on your tongue . . .

Never allow a division to sunder what you say from what
    is in your heart!

Do not say: "I have found a powerful patron . . .
Now I can play a dirty trick on someone I dislike."
No. Remember that you do not know what is in the mind of God,
And that you cannot know what may happen tomorrow.
Rest still in God's arms
And your silence will confound your enemies.

Man is the clay and the straw, and God is the builder,
Daily he destroys and daily he recreates . . .

Leave no one behind you at the river crossing
While you are lolling in the ferry-boat.

Eighth century B.C.

10.

VASE D'ALBÂTRE
A SAKKARAH

ALABASTER VASE
FROM SAKKARA

11-12.

PALETTE DE NARMER

THE PALETTE OF NARMER

13-14.
SAKKARAH
SAKKARA

LA PYRAMIDE DE DJESER
THE STEP PYRAMID OF ZOSE

BARQUE SOLAIRE ET PYRAMIDES D'OUNAS
THE SUN BOAT AND THE PYRAMIDS OF UNAS

LE SERAPEIUM
THE SERAPEUM

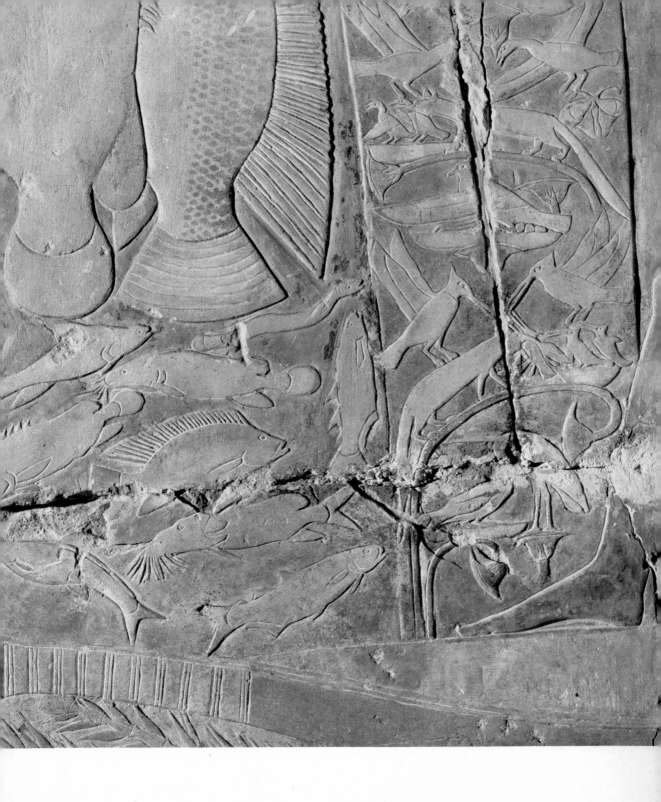

17-18.

SAKKARAH. TOMBEAU DE LA PRINCESSE IDOUT
THE TOMB OF PRINCESS IDUT AT SAKKARA

19-20.
LES CIMES DE DAHCHOÛR
THE PYRAMIDS OF DAHSHUR

21.
LA GRANDE PYRAMIDE DE MEIDOUM
THE GREAT PYRAMID AT MEIDUM

22.
MONTAGNE ARTIFICIELLE
ARTIFICIAL MOUNTAIN

23.

25.
KEPHREN
CHEPHREN

27.
ZÀOUIYET EL ARYÂN
LA GRANDE EXCAVATION
MAJOR EXCAVATION

28.
LE TEMPLE HAUT
DE MYKERINOS
THE HIGH TEMPLE
OF MYCERINUS

29.
CARRIÈRES D'ASSOUAN
THE QUARRIES AT ASWAN

30.
OBÉLISQUE A ASSOUAN
OBELISK AT ASWAN

KARNAK. LES DIEUX SONT TOUJOURS
THE GODS ARE STILL AT KARNAK

LOVE SONGS

My boat sails downstream
In time to the strokes of the oarsmen.

A bunch of reeds is on my shoulder,
And I am travelling to Memphis, "Life of the Two Lands".
And I shall say to the god Ptah, Lord of Truth:
"Give me my fair one tonight."
The god Ptah is her tuft of reeds,
The goddess Sekhmet is her posy of blossoms,
The goddess Earit is her budding lotus,
The god Nefertum is her blooming flower.
My love will be happy!
The dawn irradiates her beauty.

Memphis is a crop of pomegranates,
Placed before the god with the handsome countenance.

Nineteenth Dynasty. 1320–1200 B.C.

My love is a lotus blossom,
Her breast is a pomegranate . . .
Her forehead is a snare of meyru-wood,
And I am the wild bird
Tempted by the toothsome trap.

My love, my lover,
My heart is yearning for your love.
All your dreams,
I tell you: "Look, they have come true."

I have come to set my trap
And all the birds of the land of Punt fly down into Egypt,
Their bodies impregnated with myrrh.
The first bird that arrives darts down towards the bait.
Its body is redolent of the perfume of Punt,
Its claws are full of balm.

How I wish that we might free it together,
That I might be alone with you
So that you would hear the cry
Of my bird scented with myrrh.

Great would be my delight
If you were there, with me,
When I set my snare.

Sweet it would be to wander through the meadow
To meet my lover.

Thirteenth century B.C.

The little sycamore
That she planted with her own hand
Opens its mouth to speak.
Its rustling is as sweet
As a draught of honey.
How beautiful its graceful branches
In their greenness.
On it hangs young fruit and fruit that is ripe,
Redder than the blood-red jasper;
Its leaves are the colour of green jasper.

The love of my loved one is on the other shore.
An arm of the river lies between us,
And crocodiles lurk on the sand-banks.
But I enter the water, I plunge into the flood;
My eager heart carries me swiftly over the waves;
I swim as surely as though I were walking
        on the solid ground.
Love, it is love that gives me strength,
Averting the perils of the river.

Eighteenth Dynasty. 1580–1320 B.C.

My loved one is unique, without a peer,
More beautiful than any other,
See, she is like the star that rises on the horizon
At the dawn of an auspicious year.
She moves in a shimmer of perfection, her complexion is superb,
Her eyes are marvellously seductive,
On her lip linger persuasive words.
Never does she speak one word too many!

Her neck is slender, ample her breast,
Her hair is lapis lazuli;
Her arms more splendid than gold
And her fingers like lotus-petals.
Her robe is tightly caught in around her waist,
Revealing the most beautiful legs in all the world . . .
You cannot help following her with your eyes wherever she goes,
She is such an unrivalled goddess in appearance.

I passed by the house of the young man who loves me;
I found the door was open.
He sat at his mother's side,
In the midst of his brothers and sisters.
Everyone who passes in the roadway loves him,
He is a fine young man, a man with no equal,
A lover of rare character.
And how he stared out at me as I passed by the house!
(I was walking abroad on my own, for my own enjoyment).
And how my heart leaped up with love,
My dearest lover, when I set eyes on you!
Ah! If only my mother knew what was in my heart
She would go and visit him in a flash!
O golden goddess, inspire in her this thought!
Oh, how I wish to go to my love,
To embrace him openly in front of his family,
And weep no longer because of people's attitude,
To be happy because everyone knows at last
That he and I are in love with each other.
I would hold a little festival in honour of my goddess!

My heart is on fire with the idea of venturing abroad again tonight
In order to catch another glimpse of my lover . . .

Fourteenth century B.C.

32. A PAINTING FROM TI
TOMB OF RAMSES III

33.
KARNAK. ENTRÉE DU GRAND TEMPLE
THE ENTRANCE OF THE GREAT
TEMPLE AT KARNAK

34-35.
KARNAK
GRANDE SALLE HYPOSTYLE
THE GREAT HYPOSTYLE HALL

DANS LES RUINES DU TEMPLE
IN THE RUINS OF THE TEMPLE

36-37.
KARNAK

38-39.
KARNAK
OBÉLISQUE DE THOUTMOSIS Ier
OBELISK OF TUTHMOSIS I

KARNAK

LE JARDIN BOTANIQUE
THE BOTANICAL GARDENS

KARNAK. PROCESSION DE LA BARQUE
PROCESSION OF THE BOAT AT KARNAK

43.
LOUQSOR. LA COUR DE RAMSÈS II
THE COURT OF RAMSES II AT LUXOR

LOUQSOR. LA GRANDE COLONNADE
THE GREAT COLONNADE AT LUXOR

45.
LOUQSOR. LE DROMOS
THE DROMOS AT LUXOR

The Hymn to the Sun

By Pharaoh Akhenaton

Beautiful you rise up on the horizon of heaven,
O living sun, you who have existed since the beginning of things . . .
The whole world is filled with your loveliness.
You are the god Ra, and you have brought every land under your yoke,
Bound them in with the force of your love.
You are far away, yet your beams flood down upon the earth.
You shine upon the faces of men,
And no one is able to fathom the mystery of your coming.

When you sleep in the West, beneath the horizon,
The earth is plunged in a shadow
That resembles the shadow of death.
Then men sleep in their dwellings,
Their heads muffled, their nostrils blocked,
And no one's gaze encounters that of his fellow.
Then robbers steal into houses
And filch the valuables from beneath pillows
And creep away undetected.
The lion pads forth from his lair
And poisonous creatures bare their fangs.
Oh, how dark it is.
And what a brooding silence falls over the world,
When the maker of all things slumbers in the West!

But when the dawn comes you glitter on the horizon . . .
When day breaks, you chase away the black shades . . .
The Two Lands awake rejoicing,
Men rise up and stand upon their feet
With their arms stretched wide to hail your emergence!
The whole world then begins to go about its business.
The cattle champ their fodder contentedly;
Trees and plants open their leaves,
And birds forsake their nests,
Spreading their wings in adoration of your soul.
The young goats bound upwards,
And everything that flies and flaps its wings
Takes on a new lease of life when you smile upon it.
Boats are able to sail up and down the great river.
Your light illumines the highways and byways.
The very fish in the water cavort before you,
And your beams strike to the very depths of the ocean.

You nourish the germ in a woman's womb
And from the seed make man,
Guarding the child in its mother's womb,
Calming and soothing its tears.
You nurse and feed it before it is born,
You breathe life into the creatures you fashion.
On the day when the child leaves the womb
You open its mouth
And minister to its needs.
The chick inside the egg squeaks in its shell,
For you reach it and bestow upon it your breath
In order to make it live.
You give the tender chick strength to free itself
And to come crowing from the egg,
Standing immediately upon its feet.

122

Your rays provide nutriment for the fields,
And when you smile, they flourish
And become fruitful for you.
You ordained the seasons
To keep alive your handiwork.
You gave the winter to provide a breathing-space,
And also the summer heat.
You made the distant sky itself,
In order that you could appear resplendent there and look down
On the world you had created.
It is you alone who shine forth
In your innumerable aspects,
Whether you are but dimly perceived
Or visible in all your splendour,
Whether you are far or whether you are near.
You have created millions of things,
Towns and cities, fields, rivers and roads.
You are the focus of every eye
When you stand at your glorious zenith.

How numerous are your works,
And how mysterious to our mortal eyes!
You are the only god, you have no peer,
You made the world after your own heart,
And you created it on your own.
You made men and beasts, you made every wild and domesticated animal,
Everything that lives and moves upon earth,
Everything that spreads its wings and flies in the firmament.
You made the foreign lands of Syria and Nubia,
And you made our own land of Egypt.
You decreed every man's task and status
And made provision for their requirements.
You allotted to everyone his livelihood and span of life.

You ordained the divers tongues in which the peoples speak,
Their peculiar character
And their different colourings.
You gave individuality to the various geographical regions.
You made the Nile spring from the Lower World
And gush forth lovingly
To nurture the inhabitants of our land,
Who belong to you,
Their Lord, because of your loving kindness towards them.

O Master of all lands,
You shine out above them,
Day-Sun, mighty in power;
You have brought life to the most distant countries,
And given them a Heavenly Nile
To shed its waters upon them,
To inundate their slopes with its ripples,
To irrigate the fields between their villages.
All the mortals who have been on earth
Since the beginning of time
Have been brought up to honour your son, issue of your flesh,
Pharaoh of the Two Egypts,
Who dwells with Truth . . .
Whose lifetime is long;
And also in honour of his revered royal wife, whom Pharaoh loves,
Mistress of the Two Lands,
The Queen who lives and flourishes
For ever and ever.

Eighteenth Dynasty. Akhenaton. 1370–1352 B.C.

124

48.

LA RIVE DES MORTS
THE SHORE OF THE DEAD

49·

50.
DEIR EL BAHARI

51.

LE GRAND TEMPLE
DE DEIR EL BAHARI
ET LA MONTAGNE
D'OCCIDENT

THE GREAT TEMPLE
OF DEIR EL BAHARI
AND THE WESTERN
MOUNTAIN

55.
NEFERTITI

56.
ABOU SIMBEL
LE NIL ET LE TEMPLE
THE NILE AND THE TEMPLE
AT ABU SIMBEL

57-58.
ABOU SIMBEL
ABU SIMBEL

LA REINE NEFERTARI
QUEEN NERFERTARI

INTÉRIEUR DU TEMPLE
INSIDE THE TEMPLE

59.
THÈBES
LE RAMESSEUM
THE RAMASSEUM
AT THEBES

60.

GRAND TEMPLE DE
MÉDINET HABOU
THE GREAT TEMPLE
OF MEDINET HABU

61.
MÉDINET HABOU
MEDINET HABU

LES CHASSES DE RAMSÈS III
A HUNTING PARTY OF RAMSES III

SUR LA MONTAGNE D'OCCIDENT
ON THE WESTERN MOUNTAIN

63

LA MONTAGNE D'OCCIDENT
ET LA NÉCROPOLE ROYALE
THE WESTERN MOUNTAIN
AND THE ROYAL NECROPOLIS

VALLÉE DES ROIS
THE VALLEY OF THE KINGS

TOMBE DE RAMSÈS III
THE TOMB OF RAMSES II

TOMBE DE SETHNAKHT
THE TOMB OF SETNAKHT

66.
COUVERCLE DU SARCOPHAGE
DE SETHNAKHT
THE LID OF THE SARCOPHAGUS
OF SETNAKHT

67.
NOUT
NUT

68-69.
TRÉSOR DE TOUTANKHAMON
THE TREASURE OF TUTANKHAMON

LÉE DES ROIS
VALLEY OF THE KINGS

71.

BE D'AMÉNOPHIS II
TOMB OF AMENOPHIS II

TOMBE D'HOREMHEB
THE TOMB OF HOREMHAB

72-73

VALL
DES F
TOMBE
SETHI
THE T
OF SE
IN TH
VALLEY
THE K

75.
NÉCROPOLE THÉBAINE
NECROPOLIS AT THEBES

TOMBE DE SENNEDJEM
THE TOMB OF SENNEDJEM

NÉCROPOLE THÉBAINE
NECROPOLIS AT THEBES

76.
TOMBE DE NAKHT
THE TOMB OF NAKHT

77-78.
TOMBE DE MENNA
THE TOMB OF MENNA

NÉCROPOLE THÉBAINE
NECROPOLIS AT THEBES

LA CHASSE DE MENN
MENNA'S HUNT

83-84.
LE FAUCON D'EDFOU
THE FALCON OF EDFU

85.
COUR DU TEMPLE D'EDFOU
COURT OF THE TEMPLE OF EDFU

86.
EDFOU. LE NAOS
EDFU. THE NAOS

PLAFOND A DENDERAH
CEILING AT DENDERA

88.
PHILAE

89.

The Isle of Serpents

I will tell you something that happened to me when I went on an expedition to the royal mines. I sailed upon the Great Green Sea in a ship a hundred and twenty cubits long and forty cubits wide. It was manned by a hundred and twenty sailors, the pick of Egypt: concerning heaven or earth, they were as brave as lions, and so skilled and experienced that they could foretell a thunderstorm before there was any sign of it, and prophesy a tempest long before it actually occurred.

Well, it happened that we ran into a storm during our trip to the Great Green Sea, when we were out of reach of the land. We kept on sailing, but the storm doubled in fury, and eventually it threw up a wave that was eight cubits high. I was dealt a stunning blow by a plank, and then the ship foundered and went down with all hands.

One of the billows of the Great Green Sea took me and cast me up on an island, and for three whole days I didn't see a living soul and had to be content with my own company. I lay inert under a tree, wrapped in its shade. Then I finally struggled to my feet and went in search of food. And at once I hit upon plenty of figs and raisins, splendid vegetables of every kind, sycamore nuts, cucumbers with the appearance of having been cultivated. There were also fish and birds. There was everything that could be imagined. And at last my hunger was sated and I had to throw down most of the stuff I was carrying because it was too heavy for me. Then I fashioned a fire-stick and made a fire and created a great blaze in thanksgiving to the gods.

Then I heard the noise of thunder, which at first I took for the roaring of a breaker of the Great Green Sea. The trees were split asunder, the earth trembled.

When I finally managed to get my bearings, I found myself face to face with a huge Serpent. It was thirty cubits long, and its beard alone measured over two cubits. Its body was plated with gold and its eyebrows were made of the purest lapis lazuli. Circumspectly it came towards me.

Instantly I fell flat on my face in front of it. It opened its mouth and said to me: "Who brought you here, little one? Who brought you here? Tell me quickly who brought you here, or else I will repeat what I did a few moments ago and reduce you to ashes." To this I replied: "You speak to me and I am unable to take in what you say. I am flat on my face in front of you and I am too bewildered to understand what is going on."

So he took me up in his mouth and carried me to his den, where he put me down without jarring me. To my astonishment, I found I was safe and sound, without a scratch. He opened his mouth while I was still on my belly before him and said: "Who brought you here, little one, who brought you here? Who brought you to this island in the Great Green Sea whose two shores are in the waters?"

Then I stretched out my arms towards him and replied: "I was travelling to the mines on a mission from my King, on board a ship a hundred and twenty cubits long and forty cubits wide. It was manned by a hundred and twenty sailors, the finest in the land of Egypt. Whether they looked to skyward or whether they looked to landward, their hearts were as brave as those of lions. They were so skilled and experienced that they could foretell a thunderstorm before there was any sign of it, and prophesy a tempest long before it actually occurred. Each of them rivalled his comrades in courage and strength, and not a single one of them was clumsy or ignorant. Well, a storm broke out as we were sailing the Great Green Sea, at a time when we were a long way from land. We kept on sailing, but the storm got worse, and eventually threw up a wave over eight cubits tall. Then I was stunned by a falling plank, and the whole ship keeled over and sank, and the entire crew was drowned, except for me. And a billow of the Great Green Sea carried me to this island. And here I am, in front of you."

Then he said to me: "Don't be afraid, little one, don't be afraid. Don't look so apprehensive now that you have come here to me. God has surely permitted you to live,

174

since he has brought you to this island of the Ka in which there is no lack of anything, and which is crammed with every kind of good thing. And here you will stay, month after month, until you have sojourned on this island for a total of four months. Then a ship will come from your own country, manned by sailors whom you know; and you will return with them to your own land, where you will duly die in your own city. Happy the man who survives to recount what has happened to him, once the painful events have passed.

"I will now tell you something of what happened in this island before your arrival. I dwelt here with my fellows, our children with us. Counting the children and my other companions, there were seventy-five serpents here altogether. And I leave out of the reckoning a little girl whom I secured by means of prayer. Well, one fatal day a star fell from the heavens, igniting as it came. And it so happened that that day I was absent from home. The star fell in the midst of our little community and burned its members alive. When I found the heap of bodies, I nearly died.

"If you are strong-minded, take a grip on yourself. You will return to the bosom of your family, you will embrace your wife, you will see your house again. This is worth more than anything. You will regain your native land and your fellow-countrymen."

Then, stretched on my belly, I lowered my forehead to the ground before him and said: "I will tell Pharaoh of your power and greatness. I will arrange for many types of perfume like those which are offered before the gods in our temples to be brought to you. I will relate exactly what has happened to me in this island, being mindful of the deeds which I have seen performed through the exercise of your might. I will sacrifice a holocaust of bulls for you, and wring the necks of a host of fowls. I will cause ships to sail from Egypt laden with every kind of precious product, and present them to you as a god who loves mankind, inhabiting a far land which men have never known."

Then he smiled at me, or rather at what I had said, which he evidently thought extravagant. He said: "Many rich perfumes you lack, though the land of Egypt is endowed with resin of terebinth. But I am lord of the fabulous land of Punt, where *every sort of perfume is plentiful. Also, perfumes are among the principal products of this island. In any case, when once you have departed hence, you are destined never to see this island more. It will dissolve into the sea . . ."*

And then the ship came, as he had predicted. I was watching from a tall tree, and I recognized the sailors aboard her. When I went to announce her arrival to the Serpent, I found that he knew about it already. He told me: "Go in peace, little one, go in peace to your own home. Return to your children! See that my name is venerated in your city. I ask nothing more of you than this." Then once more I prostrated myself before him and stretched out my arms in adoration. And he gave me as a gift a cargo that consisted of all manner of rare perfumes, together with black eye-paint, giraffe tails, a huge heap of terebinth resin, elephant tusks, hunting-dogs, monkeys, baboons and every sort of highly precious thing. I forthwith loaded them all on the ship. Then, when I made obeisance to him in order to thank him, he said: "The voyage to Egypt will take two months. You will embrace your children. You will return to your country as a young man and you will be buried there." Thereupon I went down to the shore and went to the ship and hailed the crew. There on the shore I gave thanks equally to those who were on board and to the lord of the island.

At length we set sail in a northerly direction, towards Pharaoh's court. We arrived in Egypt in two months, precisely as the Serpent had forecast. I was taken before Pharaoh and I presented him with the gifts I had brought from the island. In the presence of the assembled noblemen of the whole country, Pharaoh thanked me. He raised me to the honoured rank of Companion and bestowed a number of his own slaves upon me.

Eighteenth Dynasty

176

91.
A THÈBES
A WOMAN OF THEBES

96. SAQQIYEH A GOURNAH
SAQQIYEH AT GOURNAH

97. MARE PRÈS DU TEMPLE DE SÉTHI 1er
A POOL NEAR THE TEMPLE OF SETI I

98. TISSERAND
AN OLD WEAVER

99. FEMME COPTE
A COPT WOMAN

LE BATEAU DES JARRES...
A CARGO OF JUGS...

..ET LA MAISON DES PIGEONS
..AND THE PIGEONHOUSE

106. NÉCROPOLE MUSULMANE À MINIEH
THE MOSLEM NECROPOLIS AT MINIEH

107. LE CAIRE. MAUSOLÉE DE KALAOUN
CAIRO. THE MAUSOLEUM OF KALAOUN

108-109.
LE CAIRE
CAIRO

MOSQUÉE D'EL RIFFAÏ
THE MOSQUE OF EL RIFFAÏ

112.
LE NOUVEAU GOURNAH
THE NEW GOURNAH

113.
AU CAIRE
IN CAIRO

114.
LE BARRAGE D'ASSOUAN
THE ASWAN DAM

NOTES ON THE PLATES

ACKNOWLEDGEMENTS

The authors would like to express their special thanks to the Director General of Egyptian Antiquities and to the Director of Cairo Museum for all the help that they gave.

All the plates in this book were taken by Michel Audrain, with the exception of the following:

Nos. 6, 91, 99, 107, 108, 110 (Courtesy of Hassia Photos, Cairo).
Nos. 104–5 (Courtesy of the Press Bureau of the Egyptian Embassy at Paris).
No. 88 (Courtesy of V. de Golish, Paris).

The Egyptian texts were translated from the following works:

Esquisse d'une histoire de l'Egypte ancienne et de sa culture, by Pierre Gilbert, Professor at the University of Brussels (Brussels, Collection Lebègue, 1949).
Romans et contes égyptiens de l'époque pharaonique, by Gustave Lefebvre (Paris, Adrien Maisonneuve, 1949).

COLOUR PLATES

8 THE MOUNTAINS OF GIZA. A southern view of the pyramids. From left to right can be seen the Pyramids of Mycerinus, Chephren and Cheops. In the fore-ground, in front of the Pyramid of Mycerinus, can be seen the three small pyramids of his queens. Other small pyramids can be detected on the right, in the region of the Pyramid of Cheops. Only the Pyramid of Chephren has pre-served a segment of its original facing.

9 A THEBAN PAINTING. From the tomb of Ramses III in the Valley of the Kings. About 1100 B.C.

31 KARNAK. The gods still inhabit their ancient dwelling-place. The plate shows a cobra between the legs of a fallen statue.

32 A PAINTING IN THE TOMB OF RAMSES III. This Pharaoh of the Twentieth Dynasty (1198–1166 B.C.) is shown between the ibis-headed god Thoth, god of writing and patron deity of Hermopolis, and the falcon-headed god Harakhte, one of the manifestations of the sun-god Horus. The hands of the gods are raised protectively towards the king.

46 THE GREAT TEMPLE OF ABU SIMBEL. The façade of the Temple, showing two of the colossi erected by its builder, Ramses II of the Nineteenth Dynasty (see also Plate 56).

47 TOMB-PAINTING AT THEBES. This fresco is from the tomb of a person called Sennedjem. Sennedjem, who lived under the Nineteenth Dynasty (1300 B.C.) was "a servant in the Place of Truth". That is to say, he was an official of the royal necropolis. He and his wife are shown rendering homage to Horus of the Setting Sun. The colours in this painting resemble those in the works of Gauguin, although it was painted three thousand years before Gauguin was born.

89 THE SECOND SARCOPHAGUS OF TUTANKHAMON. The wooden covering is thickly encrusted with gold leaf and with pale blue, dark blue and red *pâte de verre*. The young Pharaoh, who was only eighteen when he died, is shown holding in his hands the royal crook and flail, and on his head are the sacred vulture and the snake-symbol called the Uraeus. The whole work is carried out in a mood of Oriental luxury.

90 A CHILD AT LUXOR. Blood-royal.

205

Frontispiece.

THE GREAT PYRAMID OF CHEOPS. An aerial view from the north-east. The pyramid was called "the Shining One" by the ancients because of its dazzling casing of white limestone. The casing was afterwards stripped away by treasure-hunters and stone-quarriers. The pyramid was originally 490 feet high and its base covered an area of 31 acres. Its four faces are rigorously aligned on the cardinal points of the compass, and the pyramid possesses the most remarkable numerical and geometrical properties.

Clustered at the foot of the west face of the pyramid can be seen an accumulation of mastabas, or tombs of leading courtiers. Behind the pyramid is the luxurious vegetation of the Nile Valley.

1 EGYPT. Egypt consists of an enormous elongated oasis stretched between two deserts. The land is not only a product of the Nile, but of sun and silt. The labours of countless generations have made it one of the most fertile countries in the world.

2 A FISHERMAN IN LAKE MARIOUT. The lake is in the Delta of Lower Egypt, where the Nile's hundred arms fan out like a huge papyrus-flower. Here it voids its muddy waters into the Mediterranean. The Delta is a wide expanse, threaded with flowing streams, studded with stagnant pools, filled with reeds, breezes and flocks of birds.

3 THE FAYÛM. The Fayûm is a vast fertile basin situated on the western side of the valley and separated from it by strips of desert. Its cultivation represents a victory achieved by man over sand and stone. The victory was brought about by some of the most ancient hydraulic devices known to history. Tradition assigns the erection of the first barrages, artificial lakes and other works to the Pharaoh Amenemhat III of the Twelfth Dynasty.

4-5 THE NILE AND THE FIRST CATARACT AT ASWAN. Here is the final boundary of the land of Egypt. The band of cultivated soil dwindles to a few yards in width, disappearing a little higher up in a sea of stone and sand that is strangely reminiscent of an expanse of snow. When one visits Aswan, one is better able to appreciate the impression made on the Ancient Egyptians by the spectacle of these inexhaustible waters, surging miraculously out of the arid desert.

6 THE END OF THE WORLD. Here is the boundary of the universe as it appeared to the Ancient Egyptians. Its appearance is still the same today. The only

206

inhabitants of this desolate area are the sun, the wolves and an occasional troop of gazelles.

7 THE HILL OF THE TEN COMMANDMENTS. The land of Sinai is situated between the Gulf of Suez and the Gulf of Akabah. It calls to mind the Book of Exodus, and also the many expeditions sent there by the Pharaohs of Egypt in order to work the rich lodes of copper and precious stones. The landscape of Sinai is as dry as death, violently coloured, covered with fantastic rocky designs. A few Greek monks, successors of the original Anchorites, still live in the Convent of St. Catherine, built by the Emperor Justinian at the foot of the so-called Mountain of God in A.D. 527. The photograph shows the little plain of Rahah, where the Jewish tribes are once said to have camped.

8 THE MOUNTAINS OF GIZA (*see notes on Colour Plates*).

9 A THEBAN PAINTING (*see notes on Colour Plates*).

10 AN ALABASTER VASE. The vase is from Sakkara, and dates from the reign of the Pharaoh Zoser of the Third Dynasty (about 2778 B.C.). This magnificent specimen of ancient craftsmanship was found intact, accompanied by many more, in the galleries beneath the Step Pyramid. During the excavations conducted by J.-P. Lauer, an extraordinary number of stone vessels were discovered, perhaps as many as 30,000 or 40,000. A great number of them had been crushed by the vaults of the galleries. [*The photograph is reproduced through M. Lauer's kindness.*]

11-12 THE PALETTE OF NARMER. The photographs show the front and back of this pre-dynastic sandstone palette, which is one of the oldest examples of Egyptian art. Executed about 3330 B.C. it commemorates the conquest of Lower by Upper Egypt. The conquering Pharaoh, Narmer, has been identified with the Pharaoh who is called Menes in the Greek sources. The representation of the falcon on the palette may be compared with representations of Horus of Edfu.

13 THE STEP PYRAMID AT SAKKARA. This was the first pyramid to be constructed in Egypt. Its architect was Imhotep, Vizier of the Pharaoh Zoser, who reigned about 2778 B.C. Imhotep was a famous savant, and was later deified. This monument, together with the complex of buildings that surrounds it, is the first stone building of elaborate design in the world. Its proportions are impressive. It was 200 feet high, and its sides measured over 300 feet. It was constructed on the site of an early mastaba, and consisted of six steps with an inaccessible platform on the summit.

207

14 THE SUN BOAT. The photograph also shows the pyramid of Unas, constructed at Sakkara about 2242 B.C., during the Fifth Dynasty. Solar boats like these are found at the foot of pyramids. Their purpose is connected with the myth of the Sun God, who sailed the waters of the Heavenly Nile by day and the waters of the Infernal Nile by night.

15 REED COLUMNS AT SAKKARA. The columns are of a type unique in Egyptian art. They appear to be derived from a more primitive column, formed from bundles of reeds tied together. The form reminds one forcibly of the Doric column of the Greeks, particularly in its lack of ornamentation and purity of line.

16 THE SERAPEUM AT SAKKARA. The photograph shows the sarcophagus of an Apis bull. These huge catacombs were discovered by Mariette in 1851. They contain the enormous tombs of the bulls of Apis, which formed part of the cult of Ptah, god of Memphis. It was the usual practice in Egypt to mummify large numbers of birds and animals that were considered to be sacred, including cats, crocodiles and ibises. This custom lasted as long as Egypt itself. The tombs in the Serapeum were in use in the reign of the Pharaoh Psammetichus I (663–609 B.C.) and were afterwards utilized by the Ptolemies.

The Serapeum is one of the most impressive buildings in the whole of Egypt, due to its colossal proportions, its deep shadows, and the deathly pomp exuded by its walls. The geometrical facets of the granite tomb have been cut with astonishing accuracy.

17–18 THE TOMB OF A PRINCESS OF THE OLD KINGDOM. The word *mastaba* is an Arabic term for a bench. It has been given by archaeologists to the tombs of noblemen and great courtiers associated with the funerary cult of the Pharaohs. The visible portion of the mastaba resembles a bench in that it consists of a massive rectangle with flat top and four symmetrical sides. It is possible to compare it with the form of a cut-down pyramid.

The mastaba is an undecorated mass of stone, doubtless derived in appearance from some kind of primitive tomb or tumulus. It contains various chapels and rooms, and also a *serdab*, a narrow niche inside which the statue of the dead person was placed. At a later date, the invention of an elaborate system of mummification removed the necessity for the *serdab* and its statue.

A vertical pit, well hidden from prying eyes, descended from the roof of the mastaba for about 35–40 feet. It penetrated the interior without being connected with the various chambers and terminated in a subterranean burial-chamber.

Like the pyramid, the mastaba was orientated north and south. In the interior was a false door which always faced the east. It was in the west that the

208

sun went to rest, and through the false door the soul or Ka of the dead man was able to communicate with the living world.

The mastaba was the house of the living dead. The statue and other appurtenances were not only able to evoke the life on earth of the dead man, but also to

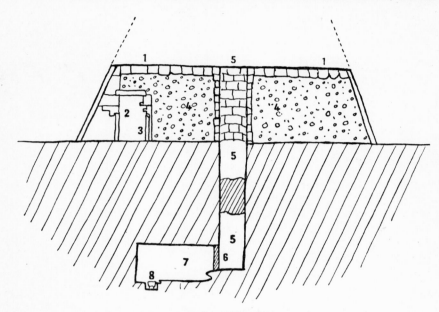

Cross-section of an Old Kingdom mastaba

1. Revetment
2. Chapel
3. Stele
4. Filling

5. Shaft
6. Sealing-slab
7. Tomb-chamber
8. Sarcophagus

provide everything he would need in the life beyond the grave. The walls of the mastaba were therefore covered with a miniature representation of the living world. Besides the scenes of everyday life which they depicted, they also showed scenes in which the household of the dead person made offerings to him. Plate 17 shows a theme in which butchers are at work, and Plate 18 shows a detail from a mural in which men are fishing in a pond. One must surely admire the impeccable style of these designs, in which scrupulous observation of Nature is united with the greatest liberty of expression.

19 THE PYRAMIDS OF DAHSHUR. An aerial view from the south. In the foreground is the Bent Pyramid of the Pharaoh Snofru, of the Fourth Dynasty. The

harmonious outline, reminiscent of rock-crystal, tends to disprove the hypothesis that its abrupt change in angle was due to an error in calculation on the part of the architect. The Bent Pyramid gives the impression of a work of art faithfully carried out according to a preconceived plan (height, 320 feet, length of side, 620 feet).

The photograph shows clearly the remains of the smooth facing which originally existed. It also shows the vestiges of a surrounding wall. In front of the Bent Pyramid is the little pyramid of Snofru's Queen. In the top left corner of the picture can be seen the great pyramid of Dahshur (height, 325 feet, length of side, 700 feet), which is also attributed to Snofru. It is thought to have been the earliest regular pyramid. The angles of its faces are not as steep as those of the Pyramid of Cheops at Giza.

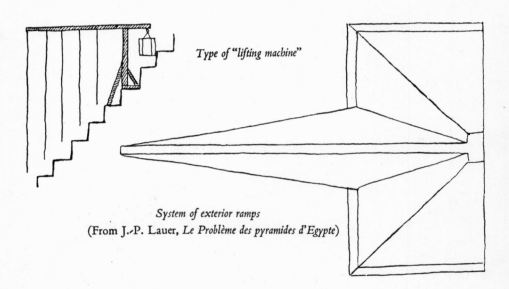

Type of "lifting machine"

System of exterior ramps
(From J.-P. Lauer, *Le Problème des pyramides d'Egypte*)

20 DETAIL OF THE BENT PYRAMID. Another view of the remains of the casing.
Casings of this type have practically all disappeared. The sole exceptions are the casing at the summit of the Pyramid of Chephren and a few traces at the base of the Pyramid of Mycerinus. The casings were demolished by thieves and quarriers. It has been said that most of the city of Cairo has been built with stone taken from the outer faces of ancient pyramids. These casings originally lent the pyramid an appearance of inaccessibility. This point is important in view of the symbolic function of these monuments.

One can clearly see in the photograph the way in which the outer casing was constructed, and the beautiful fashion in which the individual blocks are snugly recessed into each other.

21 THE GREAT PYRAMID OF MEIDUM. It would appear that this pyramid con‐ sisted originally of seven steps. It may therefore be linked symbolically with the true Step Pyramid of Zoser, and may constitute another architectural rendering of the primitive idea of a ladder or staircase by which the King‐God was suppose to climb to heaven in order to be finally united with the Sun.

22 AN ARTIFICIAL MOUNTAIN. The stone mass of the Pyramid of Cheops. It has been estimated to contain about 2,500,000 blocks of stone, each averaging two and a half tons in weight. The Emperor Napoleon once calculated that the stone contained in the Great Pyramid would be sufficient to surround the whole of France with a wall ten feet high and one foot thick.

23 THE KING'S CHAMBER. This magnificent architectural feat, situated within the interior of the Great Pyramid, follows strict geometrical laws. Its grandeur, simplicity and complete silence are more impressive than any scheme of decora‐ tion. There is no ornament whatsoever. There is not even a single inscription. There is only a polished dressing of enormous blocks of dark granite, jointed with marvellous precision. The ceiling itself is formed by nine monolithic granite beams.

The man in the centre of the photograph is leaning on the celebrated "bath" of red granite which has stimulated so many theories. Some writers have held that, since it does not appear to have possessed a cover, it could never have been used as a sarcophagus. This notion is certainly wrong, for a close examination reveals definite traces of a groove in which a cover was once embedded. The V‐shaped crack visible on the left of the sarcophagus was probably due to the efforts of early tomb‐robbers, when they broke into the tomb. The tomb was certainly violated in ancient times.

The block of stone on the right of the photograph has no archaeological significance. It was removed during the course of excavations in modern times. The opening covered by boards dates from the same excavations.

A passage with a low roof, containing several portcullises, leads to the King's Chamber. One of them never fulfilled its proper function, and is still in its original place.

Above the ceiling, two English excavators, Vyse and Davison, discovered five small cavities, placed one on top of the other and independent in structure. The last of them was crowned with a roof, formed from two massive slabs which had been wedged together. The technical purpose of these cavities may have been

211

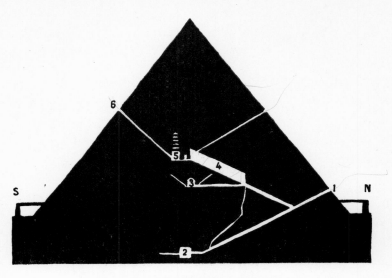

Cross-section of the Great Pyramid of Cheops
(After Borchardt)

1. Descending passage
2. Unfinished chamber
3. "Queen's" Chamber
4. Great ascending passage
5. King's Chamber
6. Narrow shafts leading to the King's Chamber

to relieve the ceiling of the Royal Chamber of some of the tremendous pressure exercised by the total weight of the pyramid. It is not unlikely that these cavities also possess a symbolic significance. It is a widespread error in the interpretation of Ancient Egyptian monuments to suppose that technical devices and symbolic meanings are mutually exclusive. It is not fanciful to argue that the architects probably desired to effect a synthesis between the spiritual and material aspects of their craft.

In one of these upper chambers were the rough inscriptions which were the only inscriptions of any kind that were discovered in the entire pyramid. They have enabled us to attribute this remarkable building to the Pharaoh Cheops. They consist of crude red-painted marks executed by quarrymen. The cartouche of Cheops is clearly depicted. It is noteworthy that these rough inscriptions were found in a chamber intended to be shut for eternity. This fact helps to demolish the old accusation that the pyramids were built to bear testimony to the inordinate pride of a succession of cruel tyrants. It is a strange pride that prevents the author of a monument like the Great Pyramid from transmitting his name to posterity.

24 THE SPHINX. The Sphinx is a lion with a human head. It represents Horus of the Rising Sun, and its fearfully mutilated face glows movingly every morning in the light of the heavenly luminary whom it symbolizes.

The Sphinx is carved from a single block of limestone, with the exception of the paws, which are of brick. Originally it was probably intended to represent the Pharaoh Chephren, builder of the second pyramid at Giza. It wears the *nemes*-headdress, a piece of material intended to protect the wig, surmounted by the royal emblem of the Uraeus. The false beard that once adorned the chin has disappeared.

In the foreground, in between the paws, can be seen a stele of granite from Aswan erected by the Pharaoh Tuthmosis IV about 1425 B.C. The inscription relates that Pharaoh went to sleep at the foot of the Sphinx, where he had a dream in which one of his ancestors begged him to clear away the sand which had accumulated around the monument. The Pharaoh carried out this pious task and raised a stele in order to commemorate the event. The Pharaoh can be seen on the stele rendering homage to the Sphinx.

Since the first rising of the sun, when Horus of the Horizon woke the world to life, myriads of men have painfully created from stone the images of their dreams, desires and divinities. But here it almost seems as if a god himself had carved a tremendous portrait of himself. No other monument has so haunted the mind of man. No other monument has invoked so mysteriously the anguish of those who are condemned to die and combined it with the inflexible serenity of those whom death cannot touch.

The ravaged visage continues to speak to us in brotherly terms. The blind eyes awake in us strange apprehensions of incorruptibility . . . they evoke in our own breasts the same dream that is hidden in the heart of this great stone being, which neither centuries nor sand, nor the endless procession of the generations of men, has ever tamed.

25 CHEPHREN. This diorite statue, now in Cairo Museum, is one of the master-pieces of Egyptian art. It is also one of the most representative examples of Egyptian sculpture. It represents the Pharaoh Chephren of the Fourth Dynasty, constructor of the second Pyramid of Giza. On the nape of the king's neck rests the protecting falcon.

26 TECHNICAL PROCESSES. This bas-relief, from the tomb of an Egyptian princess at Sakkara, gives an excellent idea of the technical processes employed in order to move the enormous blocks of stone utilized in the construction of pyramid and temple. M. Chevrier, Director of Excavations at Karnak, has made a personal test of the methods depicted. He found that it was sufficient to moisten the silt of which the soil of Egypt is composed in order to obtain a wonderfully slippery surface. On this smooth, soapy surface the blocks of stone, once set in motion, could be pushed into place by gangs of men much more readily than by any other means. The photograph shows how the manœuvre was carried out. This

213

natural lubricant must have been employed on the majority of building sites. It is so simple a method of handling difficult material that it must certainly have played a leading role in the conception and erection of the massive buildings with which the landscape of Egypt is strewn.

27 A LARGE-SCALE EXCAVATION. The sub-structures of this large unfinished pyramid at Zaouiyet el-Aryan show that the erection of such buildings was preceded by intensive digging of foundations. The T-shaped excavation revealed that the ancient architects had built the descending passage and funerary chambers from large blocks of granite. Afterwards they filled in the trenches, and the work of raising the pyramid itself thereupon went forward. Elsewhere it has been found that the descending passage and subterranean chambers were scooped out of the solid rock that served as the base of the building, but this particular feature was absent at Zaouiyet el-Aryan. It may have been for this very reason that it was decided to abandon the construction of the present pyramid, for the risk of subsidence on such a crumbling soil was considerable. On the horizon, from left to right, can be seen the Pyramids of Chephren and Cheops.

28 THE HIGH TEMPLE OF MYCERINUS. Pyramids were not isolated monuments. They represented the focal-point of a complex of buildings that was enclosed by a rectangular wall. The complex also contained a quay, leading down to the river, a Lower Temple, a great sloping ramp, a High Temple that abutted on the eastern face of the pyramid, deposits for solar barques, secondary pyramids for queens, and finally a whole village of mastabas grouped round the royal tomb itself. One can see clearly in the photograph the remains of the ascending ramp that led to the High Temple. These funerary temples were the centre of the cult of the deified Pharaohs, which lasted for many centuries after their deaths. The persistence of this worship of the dead king is a further blow to the hypothesis that the kings of Egypt were tyrants whose name was execrated in the land over which they ruled.

29-30 THE ROYAL QUARRIES AT ASWAN. At Aswan, on the First Cataract, the Ancient Egyptians quarried the huge blocks of granite from which many of their monuments were built. The transport of these blocks from the farthest point of Upper Egypt was carried out by water, with the aid of barges. The barges must have attained very considerable dimensions, since some of these rough blocks weighed upwards of a hundred tons.

The traces of such cyclopean endeavours can still be seen on the bank of the river, still as fresh today as they were when the ancient workmen were engaged on their labours. The means employed by the workmen in order to detach the individual blocks of stone consisted in making slots with their copper chisels at

214

regular intervals in the face of the rock, then inserting wedges of wood, which they moistened. The dampened wedges swelled and caused the stone to split along regular lines of cleavage.

Plate 30 shows a huge obelisk half detached from the mother-rock and left in place, perhaps because there was some defect in the quality of the stone. There are many hypotheses about the tools and techniques employed in the final stages of carving and polishing the magnificent red and black granites of Ancient Egypt, which are among the most intractable materials in the world.

31 KARNAK (*see notes on Colour Plates*).

32 A PAINTING IN THE TOMB OF RAMSES III (*see notes on Colour Plates*).

33 KARNAK. The entrance of the Great Temple, from the ancient quay.

A monumental avenue of forty ram-headed sphinxes leads to the enormous pylon outside the entrance of the Temple. The pylon was never completed. The heads of the rams are symbolic of Amon-Ra, great god of Thebes and leading god in the Egyptian pantheon.

34 THE GREAT HYPOSTYLE HALL AT KARNAK. We can see in the photograph a clearing in this vast and unique forest of stone. Each of the papyrus-headed capitals would easily provide standing-room for fifty persons. The work was begun by Amenophis III and carried on by Horemhab, Ramses I, Seti I and Ramses II. So strong is the impression produced on the modern visitor by this great Egyptian cathedral that he instinctively lowers his voice.

35 IN THE RUINS OF THE TEMPLE OF KARNAK. A colossal head of granite from Aswan, crowned with the White Crown of Upper Egypt embellished with a broken Uraeus. The statue shows the scientific command of curve and volume which is an essential attribute of Egyptian statuary. Something which is peculiarly Egyptian emanates from this particular piece of sculpture, an individual quality derived from the mysterious fusion of Upper Egypt and Lower Egypt, so dissimilar yet so indivisibly welded together. The head is a block of stone, and the block of stone is a head: yet it is impossible to say precisely where the stone abandons its appearance of stone and becomes living flesh. The whole conception springs from the harmonious conjunction of two streams of life-giving energy. One element is the stone itself, with its texture, weight, inertia and primitive power. The other is the element of intelligence, luminous, elusive and divine. In all art, the bare material and the ideal of the artist are engaged in a struggle. The artist's whole endeavour is a dramatic combat between two contradictory forces. In this example of the work of an artist of Ancient Egypt, the

215

entire creation is bathed in a cosmic peace. The quality of peace is perhaps the most profound secret of these vanished craftsmen.

36–37 KARNAK. The domain of power.

38 AN OBELISK AT KARNAK. This is the obelisk of the Pharaoh Tuthmosis I of the Eighteenth Dynasty. He ruled about 1535 B.C. The obelisk is cut from granite from Aswan, like the obelisk of Queen Hatshepsut (Plate 39) and is about 75 feet high.

   The obelisk of Tuthmosis is remarkable for its purity of line, and for the magnificent hieroglyphs with which it is covered. The hieroglyphs are executed with amazing neatness, and there is no sign of any "touching up". They astound all modern sculptors who have personal experience of working with hard stone. The Ancient Egyptians appear to have carved granite with the ease of a potter working in clay.

39 THE TIP OF THE SOUTHERN OBELISK OF QUEEN HATSHEPSUT. Queen Hatshepsut of the Eighteenth Dynasty, whose role in Egyptian history may be said to be roughly comparable with that of Catherine II in Russia, erected two obelisks in honour of her jubilee. Their proportions are rigorously geometrical. Although there is something almost sensuous about the softly-curved surfaces of the obelisk of Tuthmosis, those of Hatshepsut possess the severity of objects carved in crystal. They were probably sheathed with gold from top to bottom, and their tip was covered with gold or electron in a way which plainly indicates their solar function.

   The Queen engraved upon her obelisk an interesting inscription. It states: "I was seated in my palace, and I was thinking of the god who made me. My heart conceived the desire to erect in his honour two golden obelisks, *whose points would pierce the sky*. . . . (Our italics: The function of the pyramid is here clearly demonstrated.) . . . *venerable pillars*. . . . (Again our italics: The notion of the pillars of the sky is an archaic theme.) . . . I caused the obelisks to be erected between the two great pylons of my father Tuthmosis. You, who see these monuments after the passage of many long years, you will speak of what I have done. And you will say: 'We do not know why these needles of gold were erected.' Hearken! I lavished on them bushels of gold, as though I had been pouring out sacks of grain. And when you learn these things, do not say that my work was dedicated to vanity. Say, rather: 'She did these things because she loved to do so.'"

40 BOTANICAL GARDENS AT KARNAK. The gardens were laid out by Tuthmosis III. On the broken foundations of the walls is found a delicate carved botanical garden, teeming with birds and domestic animals.

216

41 DANCERS AT KARNAK. One of the rare representations of the acrobatic dances of Ancient Egypt. It comes from a block that has fallen from one of the pylons.

42 THE PROCESSION OF THE BARQUE AT KARNAK. Every New Year, a solemn procession left the Temple of Karnak, carrying the sacred sun-boats of Amon-Ra, Mut and Khonsu. The procession made its way to the Temple of Luxor, which served as a subsidiary temple to the Temple of Karnak.

43 LUXOR. A view from above of the court and colonnade of Ramses II and the colossi of Amenophis III. They were afterwards usurped by Ramses II.

44 THE GREAT COLONNADE AT LUXOR. The colonnade consists of fourteen columns, constructed in open-papyriform style, which still support their architraves. The lateral walls of the hall have now caved in. In the background can be seen the court of Amenophis III, and the edifice which contained the *naos* (Holy-of-Holies). Height of columns, about 52 feet.

45 THE DROMOS AT LUXOR. At the north of the Temple, in front of the great pylon of Ramses II, can still be seen the remains of the ancient paving of the *dromos* of the Pharaoh Nectanebo of the Thirtieth Dynasty, who ruled about 378 B.C. The *dromos* was the sacred thoroughfare, bordered with sphinxes, that ran between Luxor and Karnak.

46 THE GREAT TEMPLE OF ABU SIMBEL (*see notes on Colour Plates*).

47 TOMB-PAINTING AT THEBES (*see notes on Colour Plates*).

48 THE SHORE OF THE DEAD. On these same waters, thirty centuries ago, there sailed the mortuary barques that carried towards the West the mummies whose burial-rites had been carried out according to the prescriptions of Osiris.

49 ABYDOS. A bas-relief from the Temple of Seti I. The city of Abydos was the burial-place of one of the relics of the body of the god Osiris, and it became a sort of sacred shrine for pious Egyptians. It was the place where, according to tradition, the opening was situated that gave access to the infernal regions of the West. The bodies of upper-class Egyptians were often carried in sacred pilgrimage to Abydos before being taken to their final resting-place.

The temple of Seti I of the Nineteenth Dynasty was a kind of *ex-voto*. On a scale of regal magnificence, it was designed to commemorate a pilgrimage made to Abydos by the Pharaoh during his lifetime.

50 QUEEN HATSHEPSUT AT DEIR EL-BAHRI. The deified Pharaoh is represented in the customary manner, the lower half of the body mummified, the upper half represented as in life. This simple symbolism is a token of resurrection. The Queen carries in her hand the remains of the flail and the whip, the emblems of royal power (and perhaps of civil and executive authority). The terrible slash which has disfigured the work lends it a very impressive air of drama.

51 THE GREAT TEMPLE OF DEIR EL-BAHRI AND THE MOUNTAIN OF THE WEST. The great funerary temple of Deir el-Bahri was constructed by Queen Hatshepsut, and is situated in one of the most remarkable natural positions in Egypt. It was built at the foot of the cliffs of the Mountain of the West, which is shaped like a pyramid. It thus corresponds to the High Temple of the true pyramidal complex. The vestiges of a Lower Temple have also been discovered, which suggests the complete identification of mountain and pyramid. The whole temple was consecrated to Hathor, protectress of the dead.

The Temple was devoted to the celebration of the rites of the funerary cult of the Queen, her father Tuthmosis I and her brother and husband Tuthmosis III. Its architecture is obviously inspired by the landscape in which it is situated. It reflects both the horizontal lines of the geological strata and the vertical grooves of the great cliff towering above it. Its lines harmonize naturally with those of the sacred mountain: it is truly one with it. On the left can be seen the ruins of the Temple of Mentuhetep of the Eleventh Dynasty, who ruled about 2055 B.C. It formerly consisted of a pyramid resting on top of a colonnade, a form which was evidently a translation into architectural terms of the Mountain of the West itself (see Plate 63).

52 THE COLOSSI OF MEMNON. The colossi, which stand on the west bank of the Nile at Thebes, were attributed by the Greeks to "Memnon". In reality they are representations of Amenophis III, father of Akhenaton and grandfather of Tutankhamon. If one may judge by the immense scale of these "details", the proportions of the vanished funerary temple of Amenophis outside which they stood must have been gigantic. Not a vestige of the original temple remains. It may have been wiped from the earth and the memory of men by the great earth-quake of A.D. 27. Height of statues, about 60 feet.

The same earthquake ruined the upper half of the colossus on the right. This mishap led to a curious effect which made the colossus famous in antiquity. Every morning at dawn, the cracked blocks issued a melodious whistling noise, which may have been caused by the evaporation of dew in the crevices. Un-fortunately, the Emperor Severus hit upon the idea of repairing the statue, with the result that the music was heard no more. But "Memnon's" colossi still give rise to a peculiarly sweet kind of music: the music of thousands of doves which,

218

also at dawn, coo and flutter round the hoary heads of the two mountainous figures.

53 THE SHEPHERDESS OF THE COLOSSI. The face of all Egypt is mirrored in her proud, melancholy face. For three thousand four hundred years she has watched over her sheep and her colossi.

54 AKHENATON. A portrait of the "heretic King", from a stele in Cairo Museum. The Pharaoh, who abandoned the official religion of Amon-Ra in favour of the cult of the Aton, makes an offering to the Sun-Disk. The Disk sends down upon him its luminous rays, which terminate in human hands. Two of these hands hold out to the Pharaoh and to Nefertiti, his Queen, the Ankh or symbol of life. Both the Pharaoh and the Queen, as is common in the art of the Amarna period, are caricatured by the artist.

55 NEFERTITI. This unfinished quartzite head, executed fourteen centuries before the birth of Christ, is one of the masterpieces of Egyptian art. It is now in Cairo Museum.

56 THE GREAT TEMPLE OF ABU SIMBEL. The Temple is situated on the west bank of the river, on the borders of Upper Egypt and the Sudan. It was built by Ramses II (1298–1232 B.C.) and consecrated to Ra Harmakhis, the rising sun. The Nile can be seen in the left-hand top corner of the photograph. A thin band of vegetation separates the river from the bluffs which form the foundation of the desert landscape. The great monolithic temple, of overwhelming proportions, is cut from the solid rock. Three colossi from the two original groups are still standing, or rather sitting. The remains of the fourth are strewn on the sand. All the colossi are portraits of Ramses II, and beside them or round their feet crouch the diminutive statues of queens and princes. At the top can be seen a frieze of cynocephalous creatures, making adoration to the sun. Height of façade, 110 feet.

57 ABU SIMBEL. DETAIL OF THE TEMPLE. In the foreground is Queen Nefertari. Beyond is the entrance to the *speos*, surmounted by Ra Harmakhis, the god whose portrait is embodied in the Sphinx at Giza.

58 THE INTERIOR OF THE TEMPLE OF ABU SIMBEL. The immense statue-pillars show Osiris in the guise of Ramses. They are hewn, cut and carved from single blocks of stone. On the ceiling, vultures soar on outstretched wings.

59 THE RAMASSEUM AT THEBES. The Ramasseum is Ramses II's mortuary temple, constructed on the west bank of the Nile at Thebes. Its ruins are among the most moving in the whole of the Thebaid. The temple, isolated in a luminous

funereal setting, unites the usual robust characteristics of Egyptian architecture with a grace and charm that, viewed at certain hours and under certain conditions, can only be described as romantic.

The photograph is taken from a point north of the second pylon. Beyond the courtyard is a façade, ornamented with Osirian pillars that are now unfortunately truncated. In the distance is the Mountain of the West, in the face of which the openings of several ordinary tombs can be detected.

60 THE GREAT TEMPLE OF MEDINET HABU. This is the funerary temple of Ramses III of the Twentieth Dynasty (1198 B.C.). The photograph shows the remains of an Osirian colonnade on one of the courtyards. A few traces of the lavish painted decoration that once existed can be descried.

61 THE HUNT OF RAMSES III AT MEDINET HABU. The huge relief is situated in the north-west of the building, near the first pylon. Here, thanks to an artistic miracle, the stone seems to pant and shimmer. The relief is an epic film whose leading actor is the renowned Pharaoh Ramses III.

Carried along by his team of steeds, Pharaoh passes by in his chariot like a whirlwind. Troops of antelopes scatter and flee: but there is plenty of other game! Wild bulls stampede towards the swamps to seek cover, while the beaters bend their bows and loose their whistling arrows into their flanks. Heavy bodies crash blindly through the undergrowth. But Pharaoh is on the track of a fleeing beast. He draws back his arm, loosing the reins of his two plumed thoroughbreds. A javelin bores its way through the air. The beast falls with its muzzle in the water, scaring shoals of fishes away from the shallows towards the depths of the stream. Pharaoh's hunt is passing . . . Pharaoh's hunt has passed. . . .

62 ON THE EASTERN FACE OF THE MOUNTAIN OF THE WEST. The Mountain stands between two worlds. On one side of it is the world of the Nile, the world of life and vegetation. On the other side is the world of silence and baked stone.

The pits that are visible are the remains of the shacks of the workmen who once worked on the royal tombs. Their ruins are still there. And why shouldn't they be? Everything in Egypt projects itself effortlessly into the future. If you stir a pebble with your foot, it will lie in its new position for a century, perhaps for fifty centuries.

63 THE MOUNTAIN OF THE WEST AND THE ROYAL NECROPOLIS. From the Eighteenth Dynasty onwards, the Pharaohs of Egypt decided to entrust their mummified bodies to a desolate spot in the Valley of the Kings which abuts on the natural pyramid of the Mountain of the West.

At the very bottom of the Plate can be seen the mouths of several tombs.

64 THE TOMB OF RAMSES III IN THE VALLEY OF THE KINGS. The Plate shows the tomb's descending passage.

There are fifty-four known tombs in the Valley of the Kings. The largest of them, the hypogeum of Seti I, is over 500 feet long and is 150 feet below the level of the Valley floor.

Every tomb is constructed according to a different ground-plan, but all of them consist of a nexus of labyrinthine rooms and galleries. They are filled with ramps, staircases, pits, culs-de-sac and other devices designed to frustrate robbers. At the very bottom of each tomb is a chamber or suite of chambers destined to receive the royal sarcophagus.

65-66 THE TOMB OF SETNAKHT IN THE VALLEY OF THE KINGS. The tomb-chamber and sarcophagus of Setnakht, a Pharaoh of the Twentieth Dynasty, have long ago been rifled.

A heavy, oppressive atmosphere pervades the tomb-chamber. The thickness of the darkness produces an almost tactile impression on the visitor. The beam of his electric torch is immediately swallowed up by fresh banks of shadow. Almost by accident, he stumbles up a slope littered with fallen debris from the roof. The light of his torch thrusts feebly into a wall of blackness that is practically impenetrable. He has blundered into the crypt. The torchlight flits vaguely over the surface of rock-cut pillars. For some bizarre reason, their surfaces are scored and slashed.

The visitor is in one of the most mysterious and disturbing places on earth. In the centre of the crypt he can make out the outline of a great shattered shell of granite. Its lid is more or less intact, but the rest of it is literally smashed to bits, as though by a terrible explosion. A closer inspection reveals that the stone pillars are also destroyed, as if in some conflagration.

66 THE COVER OF SETNAKHT'S SARCOPHAGUS. A vertical view. One can see an incised rendering of the royal mummy, surrounded by protecting goddesses whose loving care was unable to save him from the ruthless attention of tomb-looters.

67 THE GODDESS NUT. The interior of the sarcophagus-lid of the Pharaoh Psousennes I, now in the Cairo Museum. Psousennes was a monarch of the Twenty-first Dynasty. His capital was the city of Tanis in the Delta.

The strange and splendid sculptural motif here shown is found on many other coffin-lids, and is reproduced on a large scale on the ceiling of a tomb-chamber at Dendera. The motif depicts the sky-goddess Nut, whose body was the vault of the heavens. She is always shown arched with maternal solicitude above the body of the dead man. (To obtain the right effect one should look up at the photograph.)

68 TUTANKHAMON'S TREASURE. The lovely things from the tomb of the boy Pharaoh, who was a monarch of the Eighteenth Dynasty and ruled about 1352 B.C., are now housed in Cairo Museum.

The Plate shows an enlarged detail of a decorated wooden coffer, a unique example in Egyptian art of a type of painting that resembles a Persian miniature. Pharaoh is depicted in the act of massacring the enemy of the South, the Nubians. Note the luxurious trappings of his war-horses and the amusing fashion in which the artist has shown the royal dogs participating in the excitement.

69 TUTANKHAMON'S TREASURE. A detail of the second coffin. Isis is shown pro-tecting the royal mummy.

The mummy itself was encrusted with gold, jewels and amulets and was encased in five several coverings. The first was a massive gold winding-sheet. The second was a wooden shell covered with gold-leaf and *pâte de verre* (see Plate 89). The third was a gilded wooden case for the first two coverings. The fourth was a finely-sculpted granite sarcophagus. The fifth was a series of four magnificent golden shrines, sumptuously decorated and fitting one inside the other like Chinese boxes. The fourth and largest of the shrines nearly filled the entire area of the tomb-chamber, leaving only a few inches between it and the wall.

The mummy of the young Pharaoh has now been restored to its tomb in the Valley of the Kings.

70 THE TOMB OF AMENOPHIS II IN THE VALLEY OF THE KINGS. A detail of a pillar in the tomb-chamber. The striking decoration is executed in monochrome. It shows the Pharaoh face to face with Osiris, lord of the regions of the dead. Osiris grasps the royal crook and flail and extends towards Amenophis the *Was* sceptre, a symbol of prosperity, topped by the sign of life. The ceiling of the chamber is painted blue with yellow stars, to represent the heavenly firmament, a regular feature of the tomb-chambers of the Eighteenth Dynasty.

71 THE TOMB OF HOREMHAB IN THE VALLEY OF THE KINGS. Horemhab, com-mander-in-chief of the Egyptian army under Akhenaton and Tutankhamon, usurped the throne about 1330 B.C. His tomb has come down to us in an unusually well-preserved state. For some reason it was never completed. The painters appear to have laid down their brushes only a few hours ago, and one half expects them to reappear at any moment from the shadowy corridors and resume their work at the very point where they left it. It is hard to believe that they walked out of this cold tomb three thousand two hundred years ago. One can see where one man was working carefully on a representation of the barque of Amon-Ra, planning where he was going to lay on his reds and blacks, where

222

he was going to dispose the hieroglyphic inscription. Then one glances away to the right and catches sight of a last line of red paint, beyond which stretches an empty expanse of wall. . . .

72 THE TOMB OF SETI I IN THE VALLEY OF THE KINGS. The Plate shows the ceiling of the great hall in which the sarcophagus was placed. The fresco in the tomb of this mighty Pharaoh of the Nineteenth Dynasty is a striking example of the fantastic procession of figures that flickers across the walls of these regal hypogeums. Its effect is heightened by the fact that it is in only two colours, yellow and midnight blue. It reminds one a little of Greek figure-vases. The Egyptian fresco is actually an astronomical delineation of the heavens.

73 THE TOMB OF SETI I. A side-gallery. On the ceiling is a fine painting in coppery tints of the goddess Nut in the form of a cow, her belly sown with stars. There are also two solar barques, emblematic of the sun's voyaging upon the heavenly Nile.

Here can be seen the theme of the pillars of the sky of which we wrote in the Introduction. In this case they take the form of the four legs of the celestial cow, each of them watched over by a pair of tutelary deities, while the cow's belly itself is supported by the air-god Shu.

The Egyptian artist never avoided using a daring composition when expressing his basic ideas. The religious art of the great Theban tombs is un-realistic because it is essentially symbolic. Every form expresses its own particular idea, and these word-forms are freely intermingled with actual words themselves, without any preoccupation with their natural appearance.

For this reason the Egyptian painter did not mind two boats sailing over the body of a cow. And the entire composition is so homogeneous, and executed with such pleasing ability, that we are not shocked or taken aback by these unfamiliar artistic conventions.

74 THE TOMB OF SETI I. Another example of the extraordinary *mélange* of kings, monsters, gods and goddesses that gambol in the shadows of the royal tombs. The various scenes of the Egyptian "mystery play" are drawn as a rule from the *Book of Gates* or the *Book of What-is-in-the-Underworld*. These works describe the flora and fauna of the infernal regions and give an account of the multiple hazards which the dead man, identified with his saviour Osiris, must encounter there. It is not unlikely that such literary works also contained an additional metaphysical meaning, in accordance with the love of symbolism manifested by all ancient civilizations.

Serpents or serpent-derived monsters such as dragons play a leading role in these strange compositions. The present example is particularly knotty, twisted

223

and labyrinthine in aspect. Modern psychoanalysts might profitably make a special study of these ancient figurations. What archetypal symbols they might find there expressed!

75 THE TOMB OF SENNEDJEM IN THE NECROPOLIS OF DEIR EL-MEDINA. The burial-grounds of such Theban nobles as Sennedjem, who lived during the Nineteenth Dynasty, are situated in the eastern slopes of the Mountain of the West, facing the Nile. Whereas the tombs of royalty are decorated with paint-ings devoted to the life beyond the grave, the tombs of the nobles are decorated predominantly with scenes of everyday life. This is a tradition that harks back to the mastabas of the Old Kingdom. The tomb of Sennedjem is chiefly remark-able for the freshness and beautiful colouring of its frescoes. Its walls shimmer with subtly-blended golds, ochres and dark blues. One is continually reminded of the palette of Van Gogh, and above all Gauguin.

The lower panel represents the Fields of Ialu, an agricultural paradise where the shades of the dead spent a glorious eternity harvesting fat crops. The fields were abundantly watered and gave rich yields, while the trees groaned with luscious fruits. At the top of the fresco can be seen the barque of the sun between two cynocephalous creatures in the act of worship.

76 THE TOMB OF NAKHT IN THE THEBAN NECROPOLIS. An Eighteenth Dynasty fresco portraying young girl musicians. Nakht was astronomer scribe to Tuthmosis IV.

77-78 THE TOMB OF MENNA IN THE THEBAN NECROPOLIS. Menna was another Eighteenth Dynasty nobleman.

The frescoes in his tomb are executed with a charming simplicity in ochre and reddish-brown on a light background. They depict harvest scenes and con-tain numerous vivid realistic touches.

79 THE HUNT OF MENNA. The lord Menna sails in his personal boat upon the waters of the Nile. The river teems with life. There are brilliantly-coloured fishes, crocodiles and masses of wild duck. It is the wild duck which particularly interest my lord at the present moment.

In the front of the boat, a servant eagerly points out to his master the most likely birds. He holds in his hands the victims that have already fallen into the bag. Behind, the elder Miss Menna is indifferent to her father's prowess as a huntsman. She much prefers making delicate little nosegays. Her pretty little sister dabbles in the water, while mamma, a little apprehensive at her husband's athletic exertions, is beginning to feel anxious about him. What if he were to tumble overboard, among those frightful crocodiles? The principal actor in these

224

spirited proceedings is immediately recognizable because the artist has made him taller than his companions. (Is there some connection here with the symbolism of altitude of which we spoke in the Introduction?) In his left hand he holds a brace of ducks, designed to serve as lures, and in his right he brandishes a boomerang, a weapon used by the Ancient Egyptians as well as the modern Australians. Numerous small creatures glide in and out of the thickets of papyrus, including a wild cat, intent on despoiling the empty nests of the poor ducks who fly in all directions and fall in hordes beneath the unerring blows of the boomerang. The artist has carefully recorded his patron's best hits for the benefit of posterity.

In the lower register is a conventional picture of bearers of ritual offerings.

80 THE TOMB OF RAMOSE IN THE THEBAN NECROPOLIS. This renowned person, age was the Vizier of Amenophis III, the greatest Pharaoh of Egypt's greatest Dynasty, the Eighteenth. Ramose hit upon the happy idea of decorating his tomb with a painting in which he is shown offering a sumptuous repast to all his best friends, who were naturally drawn from Theban high society. We see them supping their eternal banquet at numerous little tables. The women are young and ravishing, and are dressed in gowns obviously provided by a Theban Fath or Dior. With the most tender discretion, they gently embrace or lean upon their escorts, who are equally young and unexceptionably handsome. The elegant fashions of the Egyptian capital are reflected in the robes, collars, bracelets, jewels and hair-styles that are to be seen in the painting. They show the astonishing degree of refinement which this vanished world of Thebes attained more than thirty-five centuries ago. Thanks to an artistic miracle, their happy figures still people this ancient wall.

81 THE PYLON OF THE TEMPLE OF EDFU. There are a thousand years between the fresco shown in the last Plate and this pylon at Edfu—a longer space of time than separates us from the Norman Conquest. None the less, during this formidable span architectural forms and religious observances had contrived to remain identical. Edfu, constructed under the Ptolemies, is a late building, but the expression "late" can often be misleading in Ancient Egypt.

The reliefs at Edfu bear, however, incontestable marks of degeneracy. Here and particularly at Kom Ombo they have lost the superb hieratic quality of the Middle Kingdom and the Empire. They have become soft, slick, worldly. But the basic architectural forms have lost none of their intellectual rigour and luminous solidity.

82 VIEW OF THE TEMPLE OF EDFU FROM THE TOP OF THE PYLON. The Temples of Edfu and Dendera are the best preserved monuments of Ancient Egypt. In

225

their general lay-out they remain faithful to the earlier temples, which are now in ruins. They consist of a monumental pylon, a great courtyard with a portico, then the temple proper with its two hypostyle-halls, its two vestibules, and its sanctuary enclosed in the numerous chapels which shrouded the *naos* or Holy-of-Holies. The entire temple-complex was shut in by a great high wall that allowed access to the body of the temple only through a narrow passageway.

The summit of the pylon at Edfu is covered with innumerable *graffiti* incised there during Napoleon's ill-fated expedition to Egypt in 1799. One of them boasts: "All the names inscribed on this monument are French ones." So Napoleon's humblest trooper here felt himself the equal of the mightiest of Egypt's Pharaohs. This mania for scribbling one's name on a wall is part of the same frantic desire to go down to posterity that was felt so powerfully in the days of the Pharaohs themselves.

83 THE FALCON OF EDFU. The inner courtyard, with the great protective figure of Horus in the familiar guise of falcon. The temple, which was under the patron-age of the god, expresses once again the triumph of spirit over brute matter.

84 HEAD OF THE FALCON OF EDFU.

85 EDFU. Another view of the inner courtyard, which is redolent of grandeur and simplicity. Note the sobriety and richness of the design and decoration.

86 INTERIOR OF THE SHRINE AT EDFU. This was the most sacred place in the entire temple. It could be entered only by initiates. The shrine is still in place, although it is not shown in the Plate. It is located in the direction thrown by the shadow of the offering-table.

87 CEILING OF A SIDE-CHAMBER AT DENDERA. Like the Temple of Edfu, the Temple of Dendera is a complex monument in whose magnificence the dying fires of Egyptian genius appear to flare up for a moment.

The large fresco shown in the photograph is rendered in blue and bronze. It shows the goddess Nut, who personified the arc of the sky, clad in a robe patterned with an aquatic motif symbolic of the heavenly Nile. The sun issues from her belly, inundating with its rays a building that represents the Temple of Dendera itself, between the two Hathor-horns of the mountain. To the right, the goddess swallows the sun as it sets. The extraordinary liberty taken by the artist in his treatment of the goddess's arms is particularly noteworthy. He has boldly transgressed all rules of anatomy in order to make the arms provide a symmetrical frame for his composition.

226

88 THE PTOLEMAIC TEMPLE OF PHILAE. The little Temple of Isis once stood upon a fragrant island in the middle of the great river. It was so beautiful that it aroused the jealous anger of the evil god Seth, the Destroyer. He thereupon made himself incarnate in the engineers who came to Upper Egypt a few short decades ago to construct the great barrage at Aswan. For the larger part of the year the Temple is now submerged beneath the waters, a wraith from the pages of Pierre Loti. Its pristine glory is remembered only by a few old men and by the river Nile itself.

89 THE SECOND SARCOPHAGUS OF TUTANKHAMON (*see notes on Colour Plates*).

90 A CHILD AT LUXOR (*Colour Plate*).

91 THEBES DRINKS ETERNALLY OF THE WATERS OF THE RIVER . . .

92–93 . . . RECALLING ALWAYS THE FEAST OF MY LORD RAMOSE.

94 THE HUMBLE BUFFALO ALONE IS OUT OF PLACE. There were no buffalo in Pharaonic times.

95 MAY AMON PROTECT US! "The chariot of our lord Ramses III has nearly caused a fearful accident!"

96 SAQQIYEH AT GOURNAH. With the aid of a wooden contraption that emits the most melancholy wailing sound, an ox, ass or camel raises in pots on an endless chain the precious water of the river to inundate the thirsty soil.

97 A POOL NEAR THE TEMPLE OF SETI I.

98 A WEAVER IN THE OLD QUARTER OF CAIRO.

99 A COPTIC WOMAN OF THE FAYÛM.

100–101 A BOAT WITH JUGS AND A DOVECOTE AT MINIEH.

102 MINIEH. A man builds his own boat. As in antiquity, the modern felucca is constructed of small slivers of wood skilfully fitted and bound together. Wood has always been rare in Egypt.

103 A FELUCCA NEAR THE TEMPLE OF KOM OMBO. The Temple of Kom Ombo is the only Egyptian temple situated right on the bank of the river. This is

probably because one of the gods to whom it was dedicated was the crocodile-god Sebek.

104 COPTIC ART. The name of the Copts is derived from the word *Koubti*, the Arabic term for the descendants of the Ancient Egyptians. The Copts and the Fellahs are the authentic if debased descendants of the great ancient race. The latter are peasants and follow the rule of Islam, while the former are Christian and inhabit the towns. In not-so-distant times it was the custom to sell the Fellah labourers, who are particularly numerous in Upper Egypt, together with the estates on which they worked.

The piece of decorated stuff shown in the Plate dates from the fifth century A.D. Its style demonstrates a complete stylistic rupture with former times. Where now is the graceful conviviality of the banquet of Ramose? Yet, despite the gigantic tearing-apart of civilizations, the sources of art still continue to flow. For, after all, the aesthetic sense is an innate part of man's character. It may become enfeebled, it may even disappear for a time, but somewhere down beneath the rubble it still seeps and trickles, seeking new outlets towards the air and the sunshine. So it is with this fragment of Coptic art. Barbarous though it is, in its heavily-worked style of composition, it nevertheless anticipates in a strange way the tapestries of Lurçat.

105 COPTIC ART. A limestone fragment from the fourth century A.D., which represents a woman riding a camel. The frame consists of bunches of grapes, a favourite artistic motif of the Christian epoch.

106 THE GREAT MUSLIM NECROPOLIS AT MINIEH. This Muslim city of the dead is situated near the cliffs of the Arabic range, a little south of Minieh, on the east bank of the Nile. Away to the horizon stretch cupolas of rough brick, every one of them a separate tomb. The necropolis resembles a gargantuan wasp-nest. On certain fixed days in the calendar, the local inhabitants come to the cemetery to spend several days in proximity with their dead relatives, to whom they bring offerings of dates and palm-branches.

107 THE MAUSOLEUM OF KALAOUN AT CAIRO.

108 THE MOSQUE OF EL RIFFAI AT CAIRO.

109 THE MOSQUE OF THE CITADEL AT CAIRO. The Mosque was built by Mahomet Ali in the Turkish style. It consists of a great gilded circular room.

110 THE MOSQUE OF SULTAN HASSAN AT CAIRO. The naked mystery of the desert has been recaptured in this building. A masterpiece of the purest style of Arabic

architecture, it was constructed between 1356 and 1362. The photograph shows the central courtyard with its fountain. Also visible are the chains which once supported lamps of crystal.

111 PRAYER AT THE MOSQUE OF AMR.

112 MODERN RURAL ARCHITECTURE. This model village at Gournah was designed by M. Hassan Fathy, a gifted Egyptian architect. He has set himself the task of re-educating the Fellahs in the art of building which was enjoyed by their ancestors three thousand years ago. He looks forward to the day when they will be able to construct for themselves solid, well-equipped houses combining modern and traditional features. He has written of the ancient villages of Egypt: "Is it not astonishing that these extraordinarily picturesque and often exciting architectural forms were evolved by people living on the poverty-line? Their dilapidated condition makes it difficult to appreciate their true merit, which has led the modern Fellah to adopt new and usually undistinguished architectural forms. Our task must be to give the Fellah back his confidence and ability in his former mode of building. We want him not only to understand, but to be genuinely proud of his native creative genius."

113 CAIRO. The Nile. Feluccas. Stevedores. Ibises winging through the sky. The whole of the great city is full of contrasts.

114 THE GREAT BARRAGE AT ASWAN. Modern Egypt adheres to the ancient policy of the Pharaoh Amenemhat III of the Twelfth Dynasty. It celebrates anew the pnutials of land and river.